Simple and profound...Jean own inner wisdom, which will always guide you down the right path. Just taking the time to do these simple, brief exercises is a step in the right direction!

—**Robbin Clark**
Manager Corporate Computer Training,
Burlington Industries

Powerful! This book provides great ideas for living your dreams and really enjoying life rather than just reacting to it.

—**David Greenberg**
Author of *Thank God It's Monday! Designing a Life You Love Beyond the Weekend*

This impressive book offers a mother lode of practical tips, anecdotes, and real life examples for anyone who's committed to improving themselves. It's practical, easy to read, and it works!

—**Carol A. Hacker**
President,
Carol A. Hacker & Associates
Author of *How to Compete in the War for Talent: A Guide to Hiring the Best*

Terrific...and powerful. Wonderfully content-rich and concise at the same time. Thanks, from the inside.

—**James Hayes**
Digital Content Management Supervisor,
Home Depot

Excellent. Some of the best work I've seen on personal development. It's incisive, profound, and goes straight to the core for a lot of people.

—**Marie Kane**
President,
Kane & Associates

52 Ways to Live Success...From the Inside Out! is a years' worth of weekly tips and action steps, great quotes, and ways to focus on how to achieve personal success. It's a book you can keep on your nightstand, in your briefcase, or on your desk and can be read in small increments, but each reading will lead to big results.

>—**Robin A. Sheerer**
>Author of *No More Blue Mondays:*
>*Four Keys to Finding Fulfillment at Work*

What I like best about your book is that you're not just spouting "stuff." Each of the *52 Ways to Live Success...From the Inside Out!* gives you the problem AND the solution in the same snippet. Makes it extremely valuable!

>—**Nancy Sain**
>Senior Manager,
>Information Technology Services,
>Fortune 100 Company

A must read! Jeanne has a gift for taking abstract concepts and boiling them down into practical words so you can understand them and apply them in your everyday life.

>—**Tom Trebes**
>Regional Manager, Benefit Partners,
>Jefferson Pilot Financial

What makes *52 Ways to Live Success...From the Inside Out!* such a pertinent read is that the examples and stories come from real life coaching situations versus your typical, business book filled with theory.

>—**Greg Vetter**
>Author of *Find It In 5 Seconds*

As a business owner and career/outplacement consultant, I have found Jeanne's book to be an outstanding "how-to" guide for people from all walks of life. Managers, employees, professionals, and entrepreneurs alike will benefit. Jeanne's book is your instant "on-the-shelf" coach for success.

>—**Emory Mulling**
>Author of *The Mulling Factor: Get Your*
>*Life Back by Taking Control of Your Career*

52 WAYS TO LIVE SUCCESS... From the Inside Out!

BITE-SIZE COACHING FOR

SUCCESS-MINDED

PEOPLE

52 WAYS TO LIVE SUCCESS...
From the Inside Out!

BITE-SIZE COACHING FOR

SUCCESS-MINDED

PEOPLE

Jeanne Sharbuno

DC PRESS

A Division of the Diogenes Consortium

SANFORD • FLORIDA

© 2002 Jeanne Sharbuno
All Rights Reserved.

All rights reserved. No part of this publication may be reproduced, stored in a retrieval system, or transmitted in any form or by any means—electronic, mechanical, photocopy, recording, or any other—except for brief quotations in printed and electronic reviews, without the prior permission of the publisher.

Published by DC Press
2445 River Tree Circle
Sanford, FL 32771
http://www.focusonethics.com

This book was set in Adobe Centaur
Cover Design and Composition by Jonathan Pennell

Library of Congress Catalog Number: Applied For
    Sharbuno. Jeanne,
52 Ways to Live Success...From the Inside Out!
    ISBN: 1-932021-01-9

First DC Press Edition
10 9 8 7 6 5 4 3 2 1
Printed in the United States of America

To my Teacher

TABLE OF CONTENTS

Acknowledgements xiii

Preface xv

Foreword xvii

Introduction xix

How to Use This Book xxi

1. A Formula for Living Success…From the Inside Out 1
2. How to Identify and Eliminate What Drains You 7
3. How to Be Irresistibly Attractive 13
4. Listening to Your Inner Voice 17
5. Your Body Wisdom Speaks: Are You Listening? 21
6. Why It's Important to Participate in Flow Activities 25
7. Two Tips for Creating More Time vs. Managing Time 29
8. Three Ways to Communicate Successfully 35
9. Are You An "Adrenaline Junkie?" A Quick Quiz 41
10. Small Steps for Big Results:
    The Toddler Method to Success 47

11.	Re-Connecting With Your Creative Self	51
12.	Less is More: An Innovative Way to Organize Your Days	55
13.	Procrastination Can Be Your Friend	61
14.	The Underlying Source of Procrastination	65
15.	How to Blast Through Procrastination	69
16.	How to Bring Simple Luxuries Into Your Every Day	75
17.	The Mindset of Positive Expectancy	79
18.	Trust Yourself: Your Inner Compass	85
19.	Take That Risk! Inspiring Words to Get You Over the Hump	91
20.	Filling the Form, Step-by-Step	97
21.	How to Define Your True Success	103
22.	A Young Boy's Story for Living Your Dreams	107
23.	The Positive Effects of Counting Your Blessings	113
24.	Your Relationship with Money: Lack or Abundance	117
25.	The Goal Filter: An Intuitive Approach to Goal-Setting	123
26.	How to Acknowledge Others Often	127
27.	Tell-Tale Clues to Being Out of Alignment at Work	131
28.	An Insider's View to "What You Focus On Gets Bigger"	135
29.	Rest in Solutions: A Creative Approach to Problem-Solving	139
30.	The Joy of Moseying, Mayberry Style	143
31.	A Sure-Fire Way to Quickly Improve How You Communicate	147
32.	Twelve Ways to Take Mini-Spring Breaks… All Year Long!	151
33.	The Art of Appreciating Success	155

34.	Common Characteristics of the Perfectly Perfect 161
35.	A Personalized Strategy for Putting Yourself First 165
36.	Ease Your Way Through Career Change: An Emotional Survival Kit 169
37.	More Tools to Ease Your Way Through Career Change 175
38.	Six Steps to a Smooth Re-Entry 181
39.	Three Sources of Support for Success-Minded People 187
40.	Five Steps to Beating the Comparison Blues 193
41.	Ten Seconds of Boldness, Twice a Day 199
42.	Listen to the Messages 203
43.	The Importance of a Smile 207
44.	How to Overcome Perfectionism and Procrastination 211
45.	How to Recognize Success in "Failure" 215
46.	Two Ways to Shift Your Energy 221
47.	The Magic of Spontaneous Combustion 227
48.	What Your Mirror Reflection Is Telling You 233
49.	A Secret to Success and Happiness 239
50.	Ten Empowering Messages to Tell Yourself Daily 243
51.	A Powerful Exercise to Wrap Up the Year 247
52.	Words to Inspire…A Graduation Message 253

Additional Reading 257
About the Author 259
An Invitation 261
Index 263

ACKNOWLEDGEMENTS

It is with warm thanks and deep appreciation that I acknowledge the following people whose generosity of time, talent, and spirit helped to make my dream of writing this book come true:

To Carol Hacker, for being the angel next door who was instrumental in getting my book into the right hands, and for spending many hours proofreading.

To Dennis McClellan, publisher of DC Press, for recognizing the value of my work, and for taking a chance on a first-time author.

To Jonathan Pennell, for his creativity, patience, time and expertise in the exceptional design of this book—both on the inside and outside.

To Geoffrey Faivre-Malloy, Mary Nelson, Syble Lackey, Maeve Duffey, and Kristina Stroede, for being my biggest champions and for their numerous hours of proofreading and contributions.

To Tim Ditzler, for his unfailing support in keeping me on track to meet my manuscript timeline.

To Julio Aguirre, my dear friend and dance partner, for always believing in me.

To my clients, whose experiences and commitment to living success…from the inside out inspired much of the material for this book.

And to my parents, family, friends, and coaches whose endless support, belief, and encouragement kept me going along the way.

I thank you all…from the bottom of my heart!

PREFACE

This book is special because of its simplicity. It's invaluable because it has the potential to change the way you're living your life.

As A COACH AND CONSULTANT for more than 30 years, working with both individuals and businesses, I've found that to make change happen is simple. It may be difficult to make ourselves do it, but it is simple—if we let it occur. And that's the beauty of **52 Ways to Live Success...From the Inside Out!** It shows us how simple positive change can really be.

As you read this book, you'll find that each of the 52 Ways deals with different aspects of our lives, our relationships, and our work. I recommend that you:

- Let yourself be supported by the wisdom you find here
- Allow these pages to connect with your own inner wisdom
- Let them guide you to make the positive changes you want to make in your life—and the way you're living it
- Commit to following the simple and practical steps in each of the 52 Ways...then reap the rewards of living success from the inside out.

Thank you, Jeanne, for keeping alive your intention to become a writer. Congratulations on your persistence in reaching your goal!

—**Jinny Ditzler**
Author of *Your Best Year Yet: Ten Questions for Making the Next Twelve Months Your Most Successful Ever*

FOREWORD

CONGRATULATIONS! You've just purchased a wonderful book by a gifted author, personal coach, and seminar leader. Jeanne is one of the most qualified people in our country to guide us toward living success from the inside out.

I first met Jeanne almost a decade ago, and we immediately became friends. We discovered we were both natives of Wisconsin and grew up 50 miles apart—yet worlds apart. I'm honored to write the foreword for her first book, although I'm not sure I'm deserving of this special task, but here goes.

You, the reader, are about to embark on a fresh new journey as you turn the pages of this delightful book by Jeanne Sharbuno. It is pure and simple, yet I believe that it meets the professional as well as personal needs of men and women from all backgrounds. The titles of her chapters alone will give you an idea of what this book holds in store for you.

How to Be Irresistibly Attractive. Now that's something most people would like to know more about, but may be afraid to ask.

Two Tips for Creating More Time vs. Managing Time. If you're like me, you're tired of the same old list of "100 ways to manage your time" that doesn't work. Jeanne narrows it down to just two tips that truly can help you create more time for yourself.

How to Bring Simple Luxuries Into Your Every Day. We all enjoy luxuries, but many of us believe that luxuries have to be in the form of a diamond ring, fancy sports car, or a $300-day at a spa. In this chapter, Jeanne shares the key to simple luxuries that can make a difference for your life and those around you.

The Goal Filter: An Intuitive Approach to Goal-Setting. I've always thought setting personal and professional goals was important. However, for most of us, that's easier said than done. This chapter makes it easy!

The Joy of Moseying, Mayberry Style. Do you remember Andy and Barney, Aunt Bee and Opie? If you grew up in the United States, I bet you do. Learn how to appreciate the joy of moseying and have fun.

Five Ways to Beat the Comparison Blues. This chapter alone is worth the price of the book!

How to Recognize Success in "Failure." Some people might read this and say: "No way. How can there possibly be any success in failure?" You might be surprised.

Words to Inspire…A Graduation Message. This is one of my favorite chapters as it is written with love and a lot of heart for a young cousin graduating from high school. I wish I had received a letter like this upon my graduation. Better yet, I wish I had thought to write a letter like this and give it to a deserving graduate. But then, it's never too late.

Jeanne has done a lot of admirable things in her life so far. I have no doubt that she has a wonderful future ahead. When I think of Jeanne, I'm reminded of the Grammy award-winning song, "I Hope You Dance" by Lee Ann Womack. Jeanne Sharbuno has her arms around success from the inside out. She is living proof that success is doable and truly comes from within. She brilliantly shares her gift in ***52 Ways to Live Success…From the Inside Out!*** I am proud to be counted among her friends. Thank you, Jeanne!

—Carol A. Hacker
Author of ***How to Compete in the War for Talent: A Guide to Hiring the Best***

INTRODUCTION

I N THE SPRING OF 1998, I began writing short articles to address the similarities I was seeing in the experiences of my various coaching clients. I thought if they were having the same issues, then there were other people out there who were also having similar challenges. I wanted to find a way to reach them too, and thus the e-mail newsletter *Success...From the Inside Out!* was born. People began forwarding these articles to their friends, family, and colleagues who in turn began subscribing to my newsletter, confirming my inkling of a great need in the world.

52 Ways to Live Success...From the Inside Out! is an outgrowth of this newsletter and has been inspired by the real-life experiences of my clients, other people, and myself. Some topics have also been identified during my many speaking engagements, and other topics have come to me as inspiration in meditation, indicating that someone was in need of hearing a particular message. Whether it was someone within my sphere of influence or someone within their sphere of influence, that particular message seemed to find its way to whomever needed it at the time. Inevitably, I would receive feedback saying that the message had come at the most appropriate time.

So often people try to solve their problems by looking outside themselves for external solutions, and then become frustrated when the problem or situation keeps showing up over and over again. What they haven't realized is that they've only put a Band-Aid™ on the symptom rather than getting to its source, which lies within themselves. And that's what this book will do—help you get to the source.

Through real life examples, anecdotes, and practical tips, **52 Ways to Live Success...From the Inside Out!** will show you that to solve a problem and to have personal success involves changing on the inside first. It includes looking at things from a different perspective, reflecting on who you are and what you need, giving yourself permission to slow down and have fun, or identifying where and how you need to change a behavior, thought, or belief system. This book coaches you in bite-size, manageable pieces on how to change yourself first rather than trying to change the external circumstances or people in your life. By doing so, you'll then find that the outside will also change and consequently that your success happens...from the inside out.

This is more than the normal, traditional success book. It's a book that will challenge you to explore your inner landscape in bite-size pieces and to accept the idea that "as it is within, so it is without." It's a book that will coach you to take a holistic approach to success.

Therefore, if you have yet to understand that the key to success lies within yourself—in what you believe, think, and do—then this book probably isn't for you. It *will* appeal to you if you are an open, forward-thinking person who is committed to your growth and yearning for more meaning and purpose in life. This book is *definitely* for you if you're searching for new techniques, tips, and insights to use on a day-to-day basis that will help you achieve success in all areas of your life.

HOW TO USE THIS BOOK

52 *Ways to Live Success…From the Inside Out!* is an innovative coaching book that is concise, practical, easy to use, and easy to read. Some of the concepts may already be familiar to you, or as one of my subscribers once said, "Hmm…now that's a new perspective. It's definitely a different point of view for me to consider." And some of the concepts are repeated and reinforced in different ways throughout the book in order to accelerate and enhance your learning, growth, and success.

Each of the 52 ways has a laser-like focus on a specific topic that can be done in sequence on a weekly basis or piecemeal, depending upon what you need at the time. Each stands on its own, so you can open up the book and start wherever you want. Each has simple action steps to be practiced or applied throughout the week, which will help you integrate the message into your daily life.

The top ten benefits you'll receive from reading and using *52 Ways to Live Success…From the Inside Out!* are:

1. Just-in-time coaching
2. Ideas, tips, and action steps to easily implement into your everyday life
3. Effective, practical, proven techniques that work
4. A single, laser-like focus which makes each of the 52 ways easy to use

5. Concepts repeated and reinforced in other ways to enhance your learning, growth, and change
6. A "do it yourself" approach to change and success vs. hiring a coach
7. Ways to take control of your destiny
8. Real life examples you can relate to
9. An enjoyable and easy read
10. A variety of topics from procrastination to fun, from personal effectiveness to self-care, from reflection to action, and so much more

52 Ways to Live Success…From the Inside Out! recognizes that we are a fast-paced society, used to instant results. It has been designed to give you simple bite-size coaching so you can achieve immediate success. I like to call this book the fast-food version of coaching with each of the 52 ways acting as your three-minute coach. I hope you'll let it serve as your portable, always available, surrogate coach. If you do, may your journey along the path of living success…from the inside out be exciting, transforming, and successful. Enjoy!

"What lies behind us and what lies before us are small matters compared to what lies within us."

—RALPH WALDO EMERSON

1

A FORMULA FOR LIVING SUCCESS... FROM THE INSIDE OUT

IF THERE WERE A FORMULA FOR LIVING SUCCESS...from the inside out, it would look like this:

Being + Doing + Having = Success...from the INSIDE OUT

Many people have this backwards. Their formula for success looks like this:

Having + Doing + Being = Success...from the OUTSIDE IN

One of my clients was faithfully following this OUTSIDE IN formula when he first came to me. His goal was to make lots of money by the time he was 40 so he could then quit his job, finally do the work he loved, and live the life he really wanted. He was working long hours

> *Success happens... from the inside out.*

to pursue this goal, had a BMW and the latest toys, and yet rarely had time to spend with his wife, friends, and family. He couldn't understand why his life lacked meaning.

Many people have their priorities upside down. They get bogged down in the HAVING stage. They can't get past it to the BEING stage because they feel like they just don't have enough yet. They think that what defines their success is how much money they have, the people they know, and the things they possess.

My client is now in the process of turning his priorities around by following the INSIDE OUT formula to success. He's finding that to have a fulfilling, joyful, and successful life, it's essential to first:

1. BE
Be yourself. Know who you really are. Know what's most important to you. Know what makes you unique. Know what you do best. This introspection and clarity will take you into the second stage.

2. DO
Do those things you do best. Use your gifts and talents in a way that helps others. Touch people in meaningful ways. Leave a lasting legacy. This takes you to the third stage.

3. HAVE
Have a life, not just a lifestyle. A life oriented around what's most important to you. A life spent with those who matter most to you. A life with financial rewards for doing what you love to do.

> "*Maintaining a complicated life is a great way to avoid changing it.*"
>
> —ELAINE ST. JAMES

2

HOW TO IDENTIFY AND ELIMINATE WHAT DRAINS YOU

DO YOU PUT UP WITH A LOT? Do other people or things bug you? Or better yet, do YOUR bad habits bug you? If you answered yes to any of these questions, then it's time to start eliminating what drains you.

What drains you are the things you put up with, the things that bug you, and the things you've neglected. What drains you can be little things and big things. They can be dishes piling up in the sink, driving in rush hour traffic, a messy car, cluttered closets, or a missing button. They can also be poor behavior in a relationship, a boss who micro-manages you, an over-flowing in-box, a friend who's always late, or a job you dislike. These things are what I call the physical, mental, and emotional clutter in your life. They hold you back and are a huge drain on your energy level.

Did you know that the average person tolerates up to 100 things at a time? Imagine that each one weighs 20 pounds, and that you're

> *The physical, mental, and emotional clutter in your life holds you back and is a huge drain on your energy and success levels.*

carrying them on your back in the backpack of your life. That's 2,000 pounds you're carrying around every day!

It's no wonder then that your energy is drained and that you're sometimes irritable. It's no wonder you're dissatisfied with some area of your personal or work life. It's no wonder you can't figure out what you want and why you may not be achieving what you want to achieve. You're carrying around too much in the backpack of your life. You simply don't have the space or the capability to bring new things into your mental, emotional, and physical environment—all because your life is packed full of clutter.

Eliminating what drains you is one of the first things I ask my clients to do when we begin coaching. They are amazed at how much lighter they feel as they clear out the clutter in their lives. They recognize that when you eliminate what drains you, you free up your energy and create space for the new. You become much more available to having in your life the kinds of people, relationships, success, and work that you really want.

How do you identify and eliminate what drains you? Start by making a list of 5 things that are draining you in each of these areas: work, home, and relationships. Be specific about what you're putting up with, what or who's bugging you, and what you're neglecting and putting off. Then ask yourself this question, "Am I willing to start eliminating what drains me?" If you answered yes, then do whatever it takes to eliminate those things. This may seem overwhelming at first, but stick with it. The rewards are worth it. One by one, clear the clutter and create new space. You'll enjoy the lighter load.

"*You attract things and people of a similar vibration.*"

—SANAYA ROMAN

3

HOW TO BE IRRESISTIBLY ATTRACTIVE

BEING IRRESISTIBLY ATTRACTIVE. What is it? Is it the new millennium's version of the "Dating Game?" Or is it "How to Attract the Perfect Job," 21st century style?

Being irresistibly attractive is about energy. It's about your energy, and the energy of the people with whom you relate. We are all energy fields; energy is all around us. It's invisible, it's real, and it's very powerful. And it's your energy that directs how you live success…from the inside out. Think of it this way. Your energy extends out around you and bumps up against the person next to you. The person's energy next to you bumps up against you and your energy.

Let's play for a moment. Find someone who will experiment with you. Hold your hands about two to three inches apart from each other for a minute and feel what happens. We put energy out into the world, and we attract it back to us. Have you heard the expression, "like attracts like?" Well, what's happening right now? Are you feeling

> *Your life is a mirror that reflects back to you what you've put out into the world. Make sure you're sending out what you want back.*

warmth between you? Does it feel prickly? Is there electricity? That's your energy attracting energy from the other person. If it's true that "like attracts like," wouldn't you agree that you want to be putting good things out there so you attract good things back?

Think about someone you know who is very needy or someone who has lots of problems. What kind of people do you think they attract and have around them? Right, they attract other needy people or people with lots of problems. Because of the negative energy they're putting out, they're actually repelling the kind of positive, successful people they'd like to be around.

Notice the kind of energy you're putting out into your world. Is it positive or negative? Remember that "like attracts like." If you're not happy with what's coming back to you, then take a look at the kind of energy you're putting out there to begin with in the form of your thoughts, words, attitudes, and actions. Ask yourself this, "What can I think, say, or do differently the next time so I can attract back to me what I really want?" And then do it. Start practicing being irresistibly attractive today.

"The more faithfully you listen to the voice within you, the better you hear what is sounding outside of you."

—DAG HAMMARSKJOLD

4

LISTENING TO YOUR INNER VOICE

S UCCESS...FROM THE INSIDE OUT IS A WAY OF LIFE. So, you ask, how does one live success from the inside out? Well, it all starts with listening. Listening to what that still small voice within you is saying. That voice is coming to you straight from your heart, and it's very wise. It has all the answers, if only you would just listen to it.

The problem is that you get caught up in the busyness of your day-to-day life and all the activities and responsibilities that go along with it. You've got way too much static on your radio frequencies to be able to hear that wise voice of yours. Fortunately, the voice doesn't go away. It just patiently waits until the time comes when you want to or are forced to listen. That time may be when life smacks you alongside your head. Why wait until some crisis happens to start listening?

Begin to practice listening to your inner voice right now. Every morning this week, take 5 minutes before you start your day to sit and reflect, meditate, or contemplate—whatever suits you. Get comfort-

> *Success... from the inside out starts by listening to what that still small voice within you is saying.*

able. Don't think. Concentrate on your breathing and just be. That may be hard for you, but do it anyway. When you notice that you're thinking about your daily to-do list or what you're going to say to your boss later that morning, acknowledge the thoughts and re-focus your attention on your breath. Do this re-focusing as often as is necessary. (And if morning isn't the best time for you, then do it in the evening before you go to bed. The important thing is to do it.)

Just 5 minutes a day to get quiet and listen to your self will get your day off to a good start. You'll be more relaxed, you'll be more centered within yourself, and you may even find that the answers to some questions or puzzling situations you have will surface. It's one of the simplest and most beneficial things you can do for yourself.

Most successful people will tell you that they take this time for themselves every day. Why not you, too?

"I think the one thing I've learned is that there is no substitution for paying attention."

—DIANE SAWYER

5

YOUR BODY WISDOM SPEAKS: ARE YOU LISTENING?

A NOTHER WAY TO LISTEN TO YOUR SELF is to check in with your body wisdom. Our bodies give us messages and clues all the time about what's going on with us in the form of aches and pains, tight jaws, knots in the stomach, fatigue, or shallow breathing. What many of us do though, is ignore what our bodies are saying and instead relegate them to just being an appendage to our heads.

Here is an example of Body Wisdom:
Do you get sick to your stomach when you drive to work? Do you suffer from Sunday night insomnia? If you answered yes, then your body is telling you loud and clear that something is amiss at work. Do you ignore these messages from your body and continue to suffer? Or do you listen to them and do whatever it takes to make changes so you can look forward to your work? Doing whatever it takes may mean

> *Your body gives you messages and clues all the time about what's going on with you.*

resolving a conflict with a boss or co-worker, finding a new job, or following your dream to become self-employed.

A client of mine in transition was checking out many career avenues, including sales. Whenever she thought about working in sales, she felt a knot in the middle of her stomach. Whenever she thought about her other career options, the knot went away.

Her body wisdom was clearly giving her the message that a sales career was not the way to go. However, rather than listening and paying attention to what her body was telling her and crossing sales off her list, she continued to pursue sales as a career. Why? Because she thought it was a great way for her to make a good income. No matter that it didn't fit her personality and talents.

After going on several sales interviews, walking away from each with a knot in her stomach, and feeling nauseous after the third interview, she finally realized her body was telling her that sales wasn't the right job for her. With that understanding, she moved on to find work that brought her great joy. That's living success…from the inside out.

How do you start listening to your body wisdom? The easiest way is to begin noticing how you're breathing. Is it with shallow or full breaths? If shallow, ask yourself what's stressing you, what you're angry about, or what you're afraid of. Take 3 to 5 deep breaths (or more) to return your breathing to normal; then figure out what it's all about and take the appropriate actions.

This week, start noticing how you're breathing during the day, and listen to what your body wisdom is telling you.

"Flow means joy, creativity, and the process of total involvement with life."

—MIHALY CSIKSZENTHMIHALYI

6

WHY IT'S IMPORTANT TO PARTICIPATE IN FLOW ACTIVITIES

FLOW ACTIVITIES ARE THE ENJOYABLE THINGS we do in life. These are the activities that are blissful and timeless. We become so engaged in what we're doing that what seems like 15 minutes is really 2 hours. When we participate in a flow activity time stands still, our minds are freed up, and a space opens where our subconscious thoughts can come to the surface. Much creativity occurs here, as well as answers to questions or situations that we may have.

How often have you been mulling over a problem and just can't come up with a solution no matter how long or how hard you try to do so? And then when you do something that is relaxing and fun, the answer magically appears in your consciousness? That's living success…from the inside out, through a flow activity.

One of my favorite flow activities is ballroom dancing. I can be stressed out or bone-tired, but once I get to the dance studio and start dancing, I'm in a different world and in total joy. I walk away refreshed and ready to go again. This is just one of the many reasons

> When you're in the midst of a flow activity, time stands still, and bliss sets in; the next thing you know, it's two hours later.

why it's important to participate in flow activities.

My other favorite flow activity is writing. When I sit down to write, I lose complete track of time. As a matter of fact, I often set my timer to remind me to eat or to make sure I leave on time for an appointment. If I don't, I forget to eat or I'm late for my appointment. That's what happens with flow activities. You are so consumed by the activity that you're totally oblivious to what's happening around you.

Because we have so much going on in our busy lives, flow activities are one of the first things we give up. What a mistake! These are the activities that give us energy, that bring us joy, that are relaxing and fun. Engaging in flow activities is also another way to listen to that still small voice within. Flow activities are VITAL to our health, well-being, and success.

What about you? Think of the activities that are enjoyable and timeless for you, those activities that take you into the "zone." How long has it been since you've done any of these? They may be dancing, hiking, reading, gardening, golfing, bicycling, running, cooking, or whatever makes your heart sing. They can also be work-related activities such as programming a computer, teaching a class, or repairing a car.

This week, choose one flow activity and schedule it into your calendar. This is your appointment with yourself to play, go with the flow, and to just "be." Take the plunge today. Step into your bliss and experience the flow of timelessness.

> *"Remember that the one thing we all have in common is twenty-four hours a day. It is up to you how you choose to spend it."*
>
> —KATHY PEEL

7

TWO TIPS FOR CREATING MORE TIME VS. MANAGING TIME

MORE AND MORE, I HEAR MY CLIENTS TELLING ME how overwhelmed they are. They have lots of projects, tasks, and activities, and there's just not enough time in the day to get it all done. They rush to this meeting here and are late to that activity there. And, they don't know what to do about it other than the traditional time management techniques. Well, you know what? It's time to be more innovative.

If you want to live success…from the inside out, choose to shift your focus from *MANAGING* time to *CREATING* time. Here are two simple tips to create more time:

1. Be 10 Minutes Early to Everything

When you are 10 minutes early to everything, it allows you to collect your thoughts, relax, and take in your environment. You may think,

> *When you decide to create time rather than manage time, you'll notice a dramatic effect on your stress and happiness levels.*

"Oh, I still have 10 minutes. I think I'll make one more phone call." What happens? That phone call runs longer than you planned, and then you're late to your meeting. You arrive stressed and irritated with yourself. Those 10 minutes are a reserve of time you build in for yourself so you can respond to the unexpected, like traffic. Those 10 minutes are NOT extra, but time you've created for yourself. When you understand this, you'll notice a dramatic effect on your stress and happiness levels.

2. Say No Before Saying Yes

This is difficult for many people. Let's say someone presents an exciting project for you to do, and you want to say yes. Yet, you already have a lot on your platter. Most people would say yes anyway. Inevitably, two weeks down the road, they find themselves overwhelmed and stressed out. All because they didn't say no to something else first, which would have created the space and time for the new project.

If you want to say yes to something new, it's vital to take a look at everything on your platter and first say no to something there. Either delegate it, postpone it, or toss it. Whatever you decide, you've just created more time and space to say yes to the new project. You'll then be able to handle it with much greater ease and joy.

Success…from the inside out starts with choosing how you use your time in ways that support you rather than stress you. It's about shifting your focus to creating time rather than managing time. And by practicing these two simple tips, you will create more time for yourself. Go ahead, try it. You may be surprised at the results.

"One may be my very good friend, and yet not of my opinion."

—MARGARET CAVENDISH

8

THREE WAYS TO COMMUNICATE SUCCESSFULLY

YOU CAN PROBABLY THINK OF A TIME when you tried to talk about something important with someone where the conversation bombed, and you'd give anything to be able to do it all over again. If only you had used better words, a different tone of voice, or waited for the right time.

I know because this happened to me not long ago. As I looked back, I realized that there were certain things I could have done differently to make it a better conversation. However, that's easier to say in hindsight than do in the heat of the moment.

In talking with my clients, improving communication is always at the top of the list. Yet it seems to me that what they're really referring to is resolving conflict rather than improving communication. They can communicate just fine when there's no conflict. It's when there's conflict that things get sticky.

Mastering the art of communication is a process, and it takes lots of practice.

> *Never close your heart to others because you'll be the one who suffers.*

HERE ARE THREE WAYS TO COMMUNICATE SUCCESSFULLY USING AN INSIDE-OUT APPROACH:

1. Own What's Yours

Remember that each of you has a part and a side in the situation. Practice the principle of responsibility by taking ownership for your part and letting the other person take ownership for their part. You DO NOT need to own and take on what's theirs. Only speak what you know to be true for you rather than saying what the other person wants to hear. Know how far you'll go and don't go beyond it. Otherwise, you'll be angry because you've overridden yourself by taking on more than what you are responsible for.

2. Come From a Neutral Place

Always use "I" instead of "you" statements. You can take a time-out if things get heated and go off by yourself to think. If you're emotionally charged, it's usually something from your past that you're reacting to rather than the person in the moment. It's important to feel the anger so you can return to a neutral frame of mind. Then come back to the conversation where you can respond from a neutral place rather than reacting emotionally.

3. Keep an Open Heart

Never close your heart to the other person because you'll be the one who suffers. Resist the urge to cut away. Be patient and compassionate with yourself and the other person. Accept your different perspectives and work towards the middle ground for harmony and good relations by keeping your heart open.

Success…from the inside out involves being able to communicate successfully and responsibly. You can begin experimenting this week by choosing something you've wanted to say to someone and communicate it by coming from the three points of reference above. Practice makes perfect, and there's no time like the present to get started. Take the risk and begin to communicate successfully today.

"There is more to life than increasing its speed."

—GHANDI

9

ARE YOU AN "ADRENALINE JUNKIE?" A QUICK QUIZ

JUST AS WE USE CAFFEINE to get us going in the morning, we also use adrenaline to keep us going during the day and to get things done. Adrenaline is a form of energy and a natural drug. It serves us well when we're in danger, yet many people misuse it as a means to operate at peak level on a daily basis. They become addicted to the high that adrenaline brings. Running on adrenaline over time wears on us physically, mentally, and emotionally. Ultimately, it causes illness and burn-out. Being an adrenaline junkie is NOT the way to live success…from the inside out.

Take the Adrenaline Quiz to see if you're an adrenaline junkie.

THE ADRENALINE QUIZ

YES   NO

____   ____   Do you drink caffeinated coffee or drinks to get or keep going?

____   ____   Do you eat sugar to calm yourself down?

____   ____   Do you tend to over-promise and then rush to get it done at the last minute?

____   ____   Do you find some way to sabotage yourself or a project, yet usually pull it off?

____   ____   Do you tend to take on more than you really want because you feel you can?

____   ____   Do you react strongly to the unexpected?

____   ____   Do you find yourself getting very upset or irritated (whether you show it or not) when people let you down, miss deadlines, or do less-than-optimal work? Do you take it personally?

____   ____   Do you arrive at work rushed or already "on."

____   ____   Do you get grabbed by surprises or upsets and then not calm down for a day or more?

____   ____   Do you feel an inner rush or lack of stillness or peace much of the time?

____   ____   Are you clearly not winning at work, yet working very hard?

____   ____   Are you the kind of person who tends to find the toughest way to get something done?

____ ____ Do you drive more than 5 miles over the speed limit, tailgate, or criticize the other drivers?

____ ____ Do you tend to run or arrive late, even if it's usually not your fault?

____ ____ Do you find that you attract more problems and upsets than you feel you deserve?

____ ____ Is money currently tight and you have been working on getting ahead, but haven't yet?

____ ____ Is it difficult to focus on any one thing for more than 10 minutes at a time?

____ ____ Do you not give yourself plenty of time during the day for things that are likely to come up?

____ ____ Do you talk a lot even after people have stopped listening?

____ ____ Do you people please to the point of feeling compulsive, regardless of cost or appropriateness?

> *Running on adrenaline wears on you physically, mentally, and emotionally. Break the adrenaline habit by finding healthier ways to motivate and energize yourself.*

Copyright Coach U, 1999, www.coachu.com. Used with permission, all rights reserved.

If you answered yes to five or more of these questions, then welcome to the club. Breaking the adrenaline habit is possible. It takes time, patience, and commitment. It also takes finding healthier ways to motivate and energize yourself during your days.

Begin to eliminate adrenaline today by changing one of your "yes" answers into a "no." Stop drinking caffeine. Be 10 minutes early. Say no to a request. Ask for help. Do what it takes to start performing in a different and healthier way. Make the commitment to give up being an adrenaline junkie. Your body and emotions will thank you.

> *"A journey of a thousand miles begins with a single step."*
>
> —LAO TZU

10

SMALL STEPS FOR BIG RESULTS
The Toddler Method to Success

NOT LONG AGO, A CLIENT CAME TO ME with a large project she had to complete. She was procrastinating on getting started, pushing up against the deadline, and feeling totally overwhelmed with all that she had to do. Plus, she felt she had to get the project done perfectly, right now, and was exhausted before she even started. Sound familiar?

I reminded her of what it's like for a toddler to learn how to walk. They're often not successful on the first try. They take some small steps here, and stop. Then they take some small steps there, and stop. This goes on for awhile, until all the small steps turn into a toddler who has now learned how to walk. Mission accomplished!

This toddler is living success…from the inside out. Toddlers instinctively know that taking small steps over a concentrated period of time will result in achieving the larger goal. The same holds true for you, too.

> *Taking baby steps over a concentrated period of time results in a mission accomplished.*

You can begin practicing "the toddler method of success" right now. Choose a project or goal that you've been putting off because it seemed like too much work to accomplish. Break it down into small, manageable steps. Schedule each small step into your calendar this week. Mark off each small step as you complete it. See how much easier it is to accomplish the project or goal that once seemed overwhelming, simply by doing it in small steps.

Remember: *small steps for big results. Now, bask in the glory of your accomplishment.*

*"Creativity is oxygen for our souls.
Cutting off our creativity makes us savage.
We need to create what wants to be created."*

—JULIA CAMERON

11

RE-CONNECTING WITH YOUR CREATIVE SELF

OFTEN I HEAR PEOPLE SAY that they really are content with the way they're living their lives. Yet, they don't understand why they continue to have a gnawing feeling in the pit of their stomachs that something is still missing for them. Or that there is something they are "supposed" to be doing, yet aren't sure what it is. Or they just aren't having the fun they used to have.

In working with my coaching clients, I've found that what is missing for many of them is a connection to that creative part of self, to what they're most passionate about, to the natural gifts and talents that are unique to who they are. They are missing their creativity.

Creativity is a gift given to each and every one of us in a form that is unique to each of us. It's not limited only to the Picassos, Mozarts, or the Bill Gates of the world. We are ALL creative beings. When that creative part of us is suppressed, we are actually cutting off a significant part of what gives us great joy and what allows us our unique

> *Creativity is a gift given to you, in a form that is unique to who you are.*

self-expression. Julia Cameron, author of *The Artist's Way* says, "Creativity is oxygen for our souls. Cutting off our creativity makes us savage. We need to create what wants to be created."

Discovering the creativity we're missing can move us in directions that we might never have thought of—in the kind of work we do, in the quality of our relationships, and in how we spend our leisure time. Start bringing into your everyday life more expressions of your creativity. Add vibrant color to your wardrobe, redecorate your office, take a writing or dance class, creatively solve a work-related problem, help your child with a science project, make something special (food or otherwise) for a loved one. Doodle.

Rather than the masterpiece, go for the joy of the creative process. Your creativity wants to be expressed. And for many of you, it's crying out for expression. Listening to and following the call of your creative self is living success…from the inside out.

Choose one area where you'd like to start playing with your creativity. Even if you think you don't have one creative bone in your body, try it anyway and start small. I promise you that you'll have fun as you begin to re-connect with your creative self.

> "Things that matter most must never be at the mercy of things that matter least.
>
> —GOETHE

12

LESS IS MORE
An Innovative Way to Organize Your Days

HOW MANY OF YOU REACH THE END OF THE DAY and feel like you haven't accomplished very much? Here you've been working like a dog all day long, forgetting to eat lunch because you were so busy, and then five o'clock comes along and you still haven't gotten done what you really wanted to get done. Chances are you're spending too much time on the details or the non-essentials, rather than on what matters most, the priorities.

Let me tell you about an innovative way to organize your days so you can feel more productive and fulfilled. What makes it so innovative? The secret lies in its simplicity. Perhaps you'd rather have some high-powered strategies that include pages and pages for your Day-Timer™ or calendar in order to stay organized. But this isn't about more and complex, it's about less and simple. It's called "The Daily Three."

The Daily Three is a practice you can immediately begin to implement every single day. It's simple, practical, and doable…if you follow

> *Adopt a new mindset, not just intellectually, but with a believing heart too.*

it. It's about selecting the top three priorities you absolutely must get done by the end of the day, no matter what. These are the three things that matter most, that are the most important. They are your priorities. They are those things that if you accomplished them by the end of the day you can say, "Now today I got a lot done" and feel good about it.

Don't make the mistake one of my clients made. He implemented the Daily Three with a slight twist. Instead of choosing three priorities, he chose five. And consequently, he set himself up for failure. His desire to do more actually slowed him down and sabotaged his success. His "more is better" mindset didn't work, and he learned the hard way that the old adage "less is more" is the key to being successful when using the Daily Three.

You may be thinking this isn't anything new. Or that it's too simple so you're not going to try it. However, I challenge you to do this every single day for one week and see for yourself the results it will bring. My client will tell you that he accomplishes much more and is more fulfilled in his work when he consistently follows his Daily Three. And he gets overwhelmed and frustrated when he doesn't. Give it a try and see for yourself.

This week give yourself permission to do less and experience the joy of achieving more. It starts with shifting your belief system from "more is better" to "less is more." When you adopt this new mindset, and that means not just intellectually but with a believing heart too, you'll be living success…from the inside out. By consistently setting and following your Daily Three, you'll achieve much success over time. Take an adaptation of an old saying to heart as you begin practicing this simple and innovative way to organize your days, "A journey of a thousand miles begins with a single Daily Three, day after day."

"Everyone should carefully observe which way his heart draws him and then choose that way with all his heart."

—HASIDIC SAYING

13

PROCRASTINATION CAN BE YOUR FRIEND

PROCRASTINATION CAN BE A FRIEND AND A FOE. "But, how can that be?" you ask. "I've always thought of procrastination as a negative." Well, read on. Procrastination usually happens when you experience these three things:

1. Being overwhelmed by the size or complexity of the task or situation
2. Feeling inadequate or incapable of doing the project
3. Lacking interest in the goal

The first two have to do with procrastination as a foe, and we'll look at those another time. The third has to do with procrastination as a friend, something we don't often consider, and that's what this nugget is all about.

Procrastination is a friend when it causes you to take an honest look at why you are not starting or finishing something. This is when that still small voice within is trying to get your attention and is actually keeping you from taking action. Rather than continually being

> *Procrastination is a friend when it's your still small voice within trying to get your attention to stop and listen.*

frustrated with inaction, this is a time when it's important to listen. When you do, you are practicing living success… from the inside out. Here's an example:

A client had several goals he wanted to accomplish. One of them always seemed to go by the wayside. Every week the action steps for that goal would be part of his fieldwork. Every week he didn't get to it. After a while, I asked him if the goal was really something he wanted to accomplish, or if it was a "should." Upon reflection, he realized that the goal was something other professionals were doing in his industry, so he thought he should too. The problem was that it wasn't HIS goal. That's why he was procrastinating and why it didn't work for him. By listening to his still small voice within, he chose another goal that was much more suited to him. And, I'm sure you can guess what happened. He was successful in reaching that goal.

Ask yourself where it is you're procrastinating. Take an honest look at whether your procrastination is a friend or a foe. If it's a friend, spend some quiet time this week listening to what your still small voice is trying to tell you and reflect upon it. Change the goal, project, or task to fit who you are and what interests you. Then, identify and take the action steps necessary to reach your new goal. Now you're on your way to success…from the inside out.

*"Nothing in life is to be feared.
It is only to be understood."*

—MARIE CURIE

14

THE UNDERLYING SOURCE OF PROCRASTINATION

YOU'VE JUST LEARNED ABOUT PROCRASTINATION as a friend. Now it's time to look at procrastination as a foe. Remember, procrastination usually happens when you experience these three things:

1. Being overwhelmed by the size or complexity of the task (Foe)
2. Feeling inadequate or incapable of doing the project (Foe)
3. Lacking interest in the goal (Friend)

If I were to give you the practical steps to overcoming procrastination as a foe right now, it would only be putting a Band-Aid™ on the situation. The first step is to recognize the underlying source of procrastination. And that underlying source of procrastination is fear. "Not me, you say. Nothing scares me. I just don't have the time." Well, time is an easy and socially acceptable excuse to use when procrastinating. Yet I have found in working with clients, that time is

> *There is something very basic at the core of procrastination. It's common to everyone, and it holds you back from success.*

not the real reason for procrastinating. The real reason is fear.

Fear can show up in these ways: fear of failure, fear of looking stupid, fear of not being perfect, fear of success, or fear of taking a risk. I'm sure you can relate to some of these.

Here's a story about fear getting in the way of success:

A client is a new commercial property and casualty insurance agent. He procrastinates on making cold calls. He says he doesn't have the time because he's busy with appointments, paper work, and training. Yet the truth is, he doesn't feel comfortable making the cold calls because he's not as knowledgeable as he'd like to be with his products. He's afraid he'll sound stupid when talking with prospects, and as a result, they won't buy any insurance products from him.

Once we got to the source of his procrastination, which was the fear of looking stupid, we were able to address that fear and come up with practical steps for him to take to move through his fear.

Now it's your turn. Choose one specific situation where you're procrastinating. If the procrastination is a foe, look at the source of your underlying fear. Is it the fear of failure? Fear of success? Fear of rejection? Fear of not being good enough?

By identifying this source, you will be taking the first step to successfully overcoming procrastination…from the inside out. Stay tuned for the practical steps you can take to blast through procrastination as a foe.

"The big question is whether you are going to be able to say a hearty yes to your adventure."

—JOSEPH CAMPBELL

15

HOW TO BLAST THROUGH PROCRASTINATION

FIRST, YOU FOUND OUT HOW PROCRASTINATION can be your friend through your intuition alerting you to stop and listen. Second, you identified your underlying source of fear that has been contributing to your procrastination as a foe. And now, it's time to blast through procrastination.

These practical steps are simple, yet not always easy. You've probably heard them before, have forgotten them, and need to be reminded. And that's okay because overcoming procrastination is all part of the on-going process to living success…from the inside out. The key to blasting through procrastination foe #1 (feeling overwhelmed) is to take small steps. The key to blasting through procrastination foe #2 (feeling inadequate) is to ask for help.

PROCRASTINATION FOE #1:
Being overwhelmed by the size or complexity of the task.

Key: Taking small steps over a concentrated period of time to achieve the greater task.

Blasting Tips:
1. Choose a project or goal that you've been putting off because it's overwhelming.
2. Break it down into small, manageable steps.
3. Schedule each small step into your calendar over the span of a week.
4. Mark off each small step as you complete it.

Reminder: It's easier to accomplish the overwhelming task by doing it in small steps.

PROCRASTINATION FOE #2:
Feeling inadequate or incapable of doing the project.

Key: Asking for help from experts or management.

Blasting Tips:
1. Select a project that you've been avoiding because you're feeling inadequate or incapable of completing the job.
2. Ask for help from a manager or someone who has expert knowledge in that area.
3. Together devise an action plan for doing the project.
4. Complete steps 2 to 4 from Foe #1 on your own.
5. Go back for help as many times as you need to if you get stuck along the way.

Reminder: Successful people understand that they don't know everything and surround themselves with advisors, experts, and consultants to help them get the job done. You can do this, too.

Now it's time for you to pull up your bootstraps and get ready to blast through your procrastination. Choose a task that is either a Procrastination Foe #1 or a Procrastination Foe #2. Start putting the recommended blasting tips into place and you're on the way to blasting through procrastination.

> *Successful people know that asking for help is more than okay.*

Are you having trouble getting started with your small steps? Here's a bonus tip. Set a timer for 20 minutes. When it goes off, you can either stop what you're doing or keep going. The key is that the timer lets you know that you have the choice to stop after 20 minutes. This may sound corny, but it works. Start blasting!

"The spur of delight comes in small ways."

—ROBERT. L. STEVENSON

16

HOW TO BRING SIMPLE LUXURIES INTO YOUR EVERY DAY

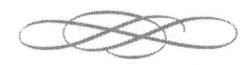

The *American Heritage Dictionary* defines luxury as:
1. Something not absolutely necessary that provides comfort or enjoyment.
2. The enjoyment of sumptuous living.

Don't you just love the idea of sumptuous living? Does that sound like a forbidden joy to you? Is it too lavish for you to even entertain the thought of luxury? Can you let go of having to accomplish, and let yourself indulge in luxury just for the experience of sheer comfort and joy?

It's important to remember that the simple things in life can give you the most pleasure. You don't have to wait for that trip to Europe, the dream house, or the expensive car to experience luxury in your life. Luxury can be an everyday thing when you think of it in terms of

> *Let go of always having to accomplish, and let yourself indulge in the luxury of sumptuous living.*

pampering and nurturing yourself in small ways, what I call "simple luxuries."

The American Heritage Dictionary says that luxury is not absolutely necessary. It's my belief that it is. It's a necessary part of taking care of yourself. It rejuvenates you when you're experiencing stress from your responsibilities. It feeds your soul. It brings you a sense of abundance. Having simple luxuries in your day-to-day life makes you feel light of heart and adds to your overall well-being. It's a part of living success…from the inside out.

Simple luxury can mean different things to different people. One person may splurge on a Mont Blanc pen and enjoy a luxurious feeling whenever he uses the pen. Another's simple luxury may be having fresh flowers on her desk to relish every week. Someone else may find the fragrance of spiced apple potpourri in their home a constant reminder of autumn in the air. You can even choose to upgrade from a simple pleasure to a simple luxury—your favorite grocery brand ice cream to Ben & Jerry's.

What are your simple luxuries? Listen to your still small voice within to hear what would be playful, luxurious, and nurturing for you. Write them down. Let yourself indulge in them regularly. There is no limit on how many simple luxuries you can have. They're the little things that will lavish you in small ways, over and over. Allow yourself the pleasure of sumptuous living, and start experiencing your simple luxuries today.

"Life tends to respond to our outlook, to shape itself to meet our expectations."

—RICHARD DE VOS

17
THE MINDSET OF POSITIVE EXPECTANCY

P OSITIVE EXPECTANCY, OR NEGATIVE EXPECTANCY? Which place do you come from? You may think you are being positive when in reality you aren't. A client once told me she went to her boss angrily complaining that her workload was unbearable and demanding immediate relief. None came. She thought she was being positive with her boss. Does that sound positive to you? If it does, think again.

Positive expectancy is a mindset. It's an eager anticipation of success. It includes and goes beyond intention, commitment, visualization, and affirmation. Positive expectancy has three steps:

1. Expecting a positive outcome
2. Doing whatever it takes for that to happen
3. Accepting nothing less

There is no room for a Plan B with positive expectancy. Plan B only waters down the positive expectation, keeps one foot in and one

> *Magical things happen when you choose the mindset of positive expectancy.*

foot out, and sets up the possibility for a less than desired result. Positive expectancy is an inner resolve that hooks up with something greater than you to create the momentum for a successful outcome.

Let's say you have a $1,000,000 sales presentation coming up. Do you go in hoping to get the sale, or do you go in expecting the sale? Notice the difference in energy here. It's the energy of your mindset that will contribute to the result. Positive expectancy is about playing a bigger game.

A client recently chose to play the bigger game of positive expectancy. As a professional speaker, she was launching a new seminar for her local professional organization chapter. They were going to do all the marketing for her. Unfortunately, that didn't happen until a week before her program. She worried that only 5 or 6 people would attend rather than the 30 she hoped for. She was already moving into Plan B to adapt her seminar to a smaller group.

I introduced her to the mindset of positive expectancy and asked her to expect to have 30 people at her seminar. To see in her mind's eye a roomful of 30 people enjoying her seminar, to keep expecting and seeing this over and over, and to eagerly anticipate a successful seminar.

My client rose to the challenge of choosing positive expectancy and as a result, her seminar was a huge success. She was amazed that it happened without the marketing she had planned on. And, how many people were at the seminar? You guessed it…30!

Magical things will happen when you choose the mindset of positive expectancy. Play the bigger game. Notice this week when you're coming from negative expectancy. Immediately shift to positive expectancy. Take a project, goal, or situation you're working on and begin practicing positive expectancy today. ***Remember:*** *expect success.*

*"As soon as you trust yourself,
you will know how to live."*

—GOETHE

18

TRUST YOURSELF
Your Inner Compass

~~~

Have you ever said to yourself:
"If only I had trusted my instincts."
"My intuition was telling me not to, but I went ahead anyway."
"I had an uneasy feeling, but I didn't pay enough attention to it."

TRUSTING YOURSELF IS A VITAL COMPONENT to living and achieving success…from the inside out. You have within you an inner compass—your internal guidance system—also known as your instincts, intuition, or gut feelings. It's the greatest tool you have, and it doesn't cost you anything. It's free and is always accessible because you carry it within you at all times.

You have all the answers inside you. However, you may often ignore the guidance you're given and go against what you instinctively know is right for you. Perhaps you're nodding your head right now, and that's okay. Because the best way to learn how to consistently trust yourself is through what you learn when you don't trust yourself and through your successes when you do. Let the following exercise help you to develop the skill of trusting yourself:

> *You have all the answers inside you. The more you trust yourself, the easier your life will flow.*

TRUST YOURSELF, AN EXERCISE

1. Think of a time when you didn't trust your instincts, your intuition, or your gut feelings. Describe this in detail. Why didn't you trust yourself? What were the results of not trusting yourself? How did it feel? What did you learn? If you could replay this situation, what would you do differently and why? What might the results be?

Ask these questions whenever you find that you haven't trusted yourself. It's an excellent way to learn and improve this skill of trusting.

2. Now think of a time when you did trust yourself. How did your instincts, intuition, or gut feelings—your inner compass—show up for you? What did it feel like? Was there an "inner knowing?" Did it feel "just right?" Was it a body sensation or an emotion? A nagging thought? A solid feeling in your body? Anything else? Describe this in detail. What were the results of trusting yourself?

Use this incident as a point of reference for what it feels like to trust yourself. Let it act as your barometer in the future when you're wondering whether or not it's your inner compass that's guiding you or something else.

Trust the information your instincts, intuition, or gut feelings are giving you. They may fly in the face of conventional wisdom or what other people think is right, but YOU know what's right for you. The key is to trust your knowing and follow it.

Your inner compass—your internal guidance system—is always giving you directions on how to proceed. The more you trust yourself, the easier your life will flow. You'll stay on course for what's right for you, and you'll experience more joy, satisfaction, and fulfillment. Remember: trust yourself and follow your inner compass. That's living success…from the inside out.

"Even if you're on the right track, you'll get run over if you just sit there."

—WILL ROGERS

19

TAKE THAT RISK!
Inspiring Words
To Get You
Over The Hump

RECENTLY I WAS TALKING WITH A CLIENT who knew she had to take a big risk in order to transition into the work she has wanted to do for years. She's at the doorstep of stepping into this new work, and it's hers for the taking. However, her fear has kept her from taking that last step over the threshold. As a result, she's stuck with one foot in and one foot out. I reminded her that both risk and change are a constant in life, especially if we want to have the life and work we love.

Here is the perfect poem for my client. Its inspiring words are just what she needs to hear to help her get over the hump. And maybe it's just what you need to hear, too.

RISKS

To laugh is to risk appearing the fool.

To weep is to risk appearing sentimental.

To reach out for another is to risk involvement.

To expose feelings is to risk exposing your true self.

To place ideas and dreams before a crowd is to risk being called naive.

To love is to risk not being loved in return.

To live is to risk dying.

To hope is to risk despair.

To try is to risk failure.

But risk must be taken, because the greatest hazard in life is to risk nothing.

The person who risks nothing, does nothing, has nothing,
is nothing, and becomes nothing.

They may avoid suffering and sorrow, but they cannot learn, feel, change, grow, love, live.

Chained by their certitude, they are slaves; they have forfeited their freedom.

Only a person who risks is truly free.

—JANET RAND

What is your comfort level with taking a risk? Does it send shivers up your spine, or do you revel in the thought of it? Success is about having the courage to take risks. Take time now to make a list of all the risks you have been avoiding or have wanted to take. Ask yourself what's been keeping you from taking them. Keep this list in a handy place, as I'll be introducing you to a concept that will make your risk-taking much easier. As Will Rogers once said, "Even if you're on the right track, you'll get run over if you just sit there."

> *Success is all about having the courage to take risks.*

"Great things are not done by impulse, but by a series of small things brought together."

—VINCENT VAN GOGH

20

FILLING THE FORM, STEP-BY-STEP

A GOOD WAY TO MAKE YOUR RISK-TAKING EASIER is to practice "filling the form." This is a wonderful tool from Julia Cameron's book, *The Artist's Way*. Filling the form means doing what comes next, which is usually something small, rather than jumping ahead to what's down the road, which is usually something much larger than what you're ready for, and where the stakes are too high. The form is the space from where you are now to where you wish to be.

Here's a personal example of the stakes being too high for me to take a risk:

> *My dream since I was very young has been to write a book. A scary undertaking for sure as I needed an idea, and the time to write it. Then I had to write it, submit it to agents and publishers, and be prepared for rejection and/or success. This seemed way too overwhelming for me, so I never started.*

> *Risk-taking is scary when the stakes are high. Make it easier on yourself by taking one step at a time rather than a big gigantic leap.*

Here's a personal example of the same story, this time using the tool "filling the form:"

My dream has always been to write a book. That seemed too much to handle so I broke it down into something simpler: a weekly newsletter. Paper and postage were an expense so I broke it down into something simpler: a weekly e-mail newsletter. Rather than racking my brain for ideas, I paid attention to what life issues came up during the week and took my ideas from them. Then, I wrote my article for that week's newsletter. When I was finished, I repeated this process week after week.

Over a 20-week period, I had written 20 newsletter articles. Over time, I had 52. The next step was to complete the process of converting these articles into a book called **52 Ways to Live Success…From the Inside Out!**

With that done, my dream became a reality. And you're holding that dream in your hands right now. All from filling the form by taking the bigger risk, breaking it down into manageable baby steps, and taking those steps over time on a consistent basis.

Now it's your turn. Choose a risk you've wanted to take, either big or small. It can be a creative risk, a business risk, or a relationship risk. Start filling the form by:

1. Looking at where you are now and where you want to be.
2. Breaking the risk down into small manageable baby steps.
3. Deciding to take each small step consistently over time.
4. Breaking it down into even smaller steps, if it's still too much of a stretch.

Filling the form is a tool that gives you a sense of comfort, order, and do-ability when taking a risk. It works. And, I can definitely testify to that.

Keep this tool handy in your tool kit—ready to be taken out at a moment's notice when you want to take a risk or fulfill a dream. Begin filling the form today, and before you know it, your risk or dream will become a reality.

*"If you don't change your direction,
you're likely to end up where you are going."*

—CHINESE PROVERB

21

HOW TO DEFINE YOUR TRUE SUCCESS

WHOSE SUCCESS ARE YOU LIVING? Is it yours, or is it someone else's? Someone else might be your family, society, the media, teachers, employers. If you're living someone else's definition of success, then it's not True Success.

Have you heard the story about the man who dreamed about being the president of a large corporation? When he was growing up, he received the message that the way to be successful and have a lot of money was to become president of a large corporation. All his life, he did what he had to do to climb up the ladder of success. Then one day he became president. And, guess what? He was miserable, tired, and burned out. He wasn't having any fun. He didn't like being president. He found that his ladder of success was leaning up against the wrong building. He was not living his True Success.

Maybe you find yourself with your success ladder leaning up against the wrong building. Or perhaps it was the right building for a while, but now it no longer fits who you are. Or maybe you know of

> *If you are living someone else's definition of success, then it's not True Success.*

someone close to you who is experiencing this.

How do you begin moving your ladder of success to the building of your dreams? You begin by taking the time to define True Success. That's what one of my career transition clients did. Her personal definition of True Success is, "Success is a process and a feeling; it's a warm glowing feeling inside about who I am, what I do, and how I'm living."

Now it's your turn. This week, set aside a window of time just for you and answer these questions:

1. What does success mean to you?
2. What do you really want in your life?
3. What, above all else, is most important to you?

Then, take the essence of all these answers and put them into a single statement. This statement is your definition of True Success. It's what living success…from the inside out means to you. Keep this statement in front of you. It will act as your guide while you move along your path of True Success.

"You are never given a dream without also the power to make it true."

—RICHARD BACH

22

A YOUNG BOY'S STORY FOR LIVING YOUR DREAMS

PETEY WAS AN 8-YEAR OLD BOY dying of cystic fibrosis in the *Touched by an Angel* episode called *Psalm 151* (originally broadcast by CBS). He had an immediate mission to fulfill his deepest dreams before he died. It was important to him to identify and accomplish these dreams so he could be at peace. With the help of others, he was able to cross off his list, one by one, the following dreams:

1. Learn how to play the piano.
2. Arrange for his friend Cornelia (a.k.a. Celine) to meet her idol, Celine Dion.
3. Inspire his mother to finish writing and then sing *The 151st Psalm*, the song she began to write on the day he was born.
4. Find a good home for his pet iguana, Fluffy.
5. Put up a tall flagpole in his front yard.

> *Your dreams will continue to call out to you, either softly or loudly, until you acknowledge them and express them in your everyday life.*

6. Make a flag for the flagpole so the angels could find him.
7. Go to heaven.

Petey's dreams were simple and profound. They came straight from his heart, as do our own dreams. And unlike Petey who had only a short time to do what was most important to him, we have a whole lifetime. Unfortunately, this luxury of having a whole lifetime often ends up with us postponing our dreams. As a matter of fact, many of us have forgotten what our dreams are, much less fulfilled them, because we've gotten so caught up in our day-to-day living. What happens then is that our future suddenly catches up with us, and we find that our life may not be quite what we had hoped for or expected.

Don't let time get away from you. What does your dream list look like? Start on it right now. Set aside the busyness and noise of everyday life. Be thankful you have a lifetime rather than a short time. Get still every day and move into the deep essence of your being through reflection, meditation, or contemplation. Ask yourself what you absolutely must do in your lifetime to be fulfilled.

Listen carefully for the answers. What you'll hear are your soul messages—those dreams, gifts, talents, and wishes that want to be expressed. They will continue to call out to you, either softly or loudly, until you acknowledge them and express them in your everyday life. It isn't always easy to hear your deepest desires. Yet by continuing to go within and listening, they will be revealed to you. This is living success…from the inside out.

Petey accomplished his dreams through the help of his inner strength, the support of others, and his Higher Power. You can accomplish your dreams with this same kind of help from a trusted friend, a coach, a family member, and/or your spiritual connection. Just as the courageous Petey found peace and joy once his dreams were identified and fulfilled, so too will you find peace and fulfillment as you courageously move into the joy of uncovering and living your dreams.

"Whatever you appreciate and give thanks for will increase in your life."

—SANAYA ROMAN

23

THE POSITIVE EFFECTS OF COUNTING YOUR BLESSINGS

WOULD YOU PREFER TO FOCUS ON blessings and gratitude or on scarcity and negativity? If you're like most of us, you'll want to answer blessings and gratitude. However, if you were to take a good hard look at yourself, do you find (much to your chagrin) that your attention is on scarcity and negativity more than you'd like it to be?

When you put your attention on scarcity and negativity, that's how you're going to experience your days. No matter what the positive is in your life, it will shrink in size as long as you focus on the negative. Imagine what would happen, though, if you would put your attention on your blessings. It would have a dramatic effect on your energy level and sense of joy. You would shift from being heavy and negative to being light and positive.

> *Count your blessings regularly and watch the positive in your life expand.*

Blessings are those things that contribute to your happiness. They come to you daily in many different ways. Some of these blessings are obvious—good health, work you enjoy, people who love you, a country that is free, a safe place to live. And some are quite subtle—leaves radiating their colors on a bright sunny fall day, a cheery smile from a stranger, the sweetness of a small child, a co-worker surprising you with a cup of your favorite gourmet coffee…just at the time you needed it.

Gratitude is giving thanks and showing appreciation for all the blessings that come your way. Gratitude opens your heart so you can feel lighter and happier. Gratitude opens you up to more joy. It's a higher call to the Universe to give you more—more abundance, more love, more peace. Sanaya Roman says in her book, *Living with Joy*, "Whatever you appreciate and give thanks for will increase in your life."

Make every day of the week Thanksgiving by acknowledging your blessings and showing your gratitude. Every night before you go to bed, mentally give thanks for 10 blessings from your day. The effects of this nightly practice will be more than you can imagine and will contribute to your living success…from the inside out.

Remember to put your focus on blessings and gratitude. Count your blessings regularly and watch the positive in your life expand.

"The law of life is abundance, not poverty."

—JOSEPH MURPHY

24

YOUR RELATIONSHIP WITH MONEY
Lack or Abundance

WHAT IS YOUR RELATIONSHIP WITH MONEY? Is it one of lack or abundance? Whichever it is, whatever you focus on is exactly what you'll get back.

It's your thoughts and beliefs that determine your relationship with money. Like attracts like. And, what you think about comes about. That's a natural law. If you focus on not having enough money, then you continue to have not enough money. If you focus on having abundance in your life, then you'll have more money and abundance in your life.

My client, Marta, came to me for coaching because she wanted to find a new job. The problem was that she thought she couldn't find work she loved that would pay her the kind of money she wanted. She kept worrying about how little she was currently making, saying there were more bills than money coming in each month. She worried so

> *Your thoughts and beliefs determine your relationship with money. What you think about comes about. That's a natural law.*

much about money that it became scary for her to even pay her bills.

It became clear to me that what Marta needed was coaching on how to shift her prosperity consciousness from lack to abundance, rather than focusing on just finding a new job. No matter how much she would have made in her new job, she would have continued to not have enough money. Why? Because her thoughts and beliefs centered around a lack of money.

Here's what Marta did to change her relationship with money:

1. She read *The Dynamic Laws of Prosperity* by Catherine Ponder and began to practice its principles. She made a conscious effort to stop herself when thoughts of lack and scarcity popped up. "How the heck am I going to pay all these bills?" or "How can I make more money fast?" And to repeat affirmations instead, "I am finding the money I need" or "Money is becoming abundant in my life."

2. She noticed how prosperity appeared in her life, whether in the form of money or in other ways, and gave appreciation for it. For instance, she unexpectedly received a refund on a deposit. Her boss gave her free tickets to the symphony. A friend decided to pay her airfare as a birthday gift so she could come to visit.

3. She thought of a part-time business she could do easily and with little start-up investment. The next thing she knew, she was hired for a weekend event doing the fun creative work she loved and getting paid for it, too.

When Marta changed her focus and began thinking about the prosperity and abundance already in her life, she started to receive more of it. She was literally transforming her relationship with money through changing her thoughts and attention from lack to abundance.

We often think that in order to make more money, we have to do certain things in our external world to make that happen—like find a new job that pays more, get a part-time job, begin investing. And then, much to our dismay, we find that by doing these things, we still don't seem to have enough money. The truth is, what you really need to do is change your internal world first. This is living success…from the inside out.

And that's exactly what Marta did. She changed her thoughts on the inside, raised her prosperity consciousness, and then magical things began to happen for her around money and abundance. If you want to improve your relationship with money, do what Marta did: raise your prosperity consciousness and enjoy the fruits of your thoughts.

> "What you get by achieving your goals is not as important as what you become by achieving your goals."
>
> —ZIG ZIGLAR

25

THE GOAL FILTER
An Intuitive Approach To Goal-Setting

HOW DO YOU APPROACH SETTING GOALS? For some, this is an easy process. For others, it's more difficult. How do you know if you're choosing the right goals for yourself in areas such as career, relationships, fun, and adventure? One way to know is by using the "Goal Filter." This is a type of intuitive goal-setting where you are choosing your goals…from the inside out.

The Goal Filter is a simple, quick tool to use that bypasses the mind and goes directly to your heart. It allows you to intuitively check out up front whether the goal you set is right for you. By using the Goal Filter, you can save yourself a lot of time and energy because it keeps unsatisfying goals at bay. It consists of two questions:

1. "When I think of reaching this goal, do I feel heavy, trapped, and/or overwhelmed?"
If you answered yes, then you know this goal isn't right for you. It's probably a "should" goal that you've bought into based on the

> *Intuitive goal-setting is a direct communication from a deep, wise place within you that knows what your heart truly desires.*

expectations that others have for you. This is a goal to quickly discard or to take back to the drawing board for fine-tuning until it fits who you are. If you don't, you'll struggle to reach this goal and will feel empty or unfulfilled when you do because it wasn't what you really wanted.

2. **"When I think of reaching this goal, do I feel light, expansive, and/or inspired?"**

If you answered yes, then you know it's a keeper. I call this a "heart" goal. This is a goal that's based on your values, those things that are most important to you. You will reach this goal with greater ease because it's an expression of what you truly want. Accomplishing this goal will bring you deep fulfillment, joy, and satisfaction.

Paying attention to what you feel and trusting what you feel—while asking yourself the above two questions—are key to the effectiveness of the Goal Filter. What you feel is your intuition talking to you—a direct communication from a very deep wise place within you. It knows what's right and wrong for you. By using the Goal Filter, you'll be able to discard those goals that aren't right for you and keep those that are.

Begin using intuitive goal-setting today. Take the goals you've set and run them by the Goal Filter. Remember to listen to and trust what your intuition is telling you. Your reward for doing so will be goals that truly are your heart's desire. Use the Goal Filter often to choose your goals…from the inside out.

"If your lips can speak a word of encouragement to a fellow soul, you have a talent."

—EVA J. CUMMINGS

26

HOW TO ACKNOWLEDGE OTHERS OFTEN

NOT LONG AGO, TWO CLIENTS brought up the same situation in different contexts. One is the owner of a small business who said she doesn't acknowledge her employees enough for all the good they do. She focuses more on what's not working well. The other client is an upper level manager in a large corporation. She said she was glad I validated what she had been thinking because she doesn't get this kind of acknowledgement in her work environment.

Whether at work, in our families, or with friends, most of us don't give and receive enough acknowledgements in our daily lives. Acknowledgements are different from compliments. A compliment is about you and your opinion, "I really enjoyed your speech today" or "I like the colors you've chosen to decorate your house." Whereas acknowledgements are about the other person and who they are, "Your courage to remain committed to your dream is inspiring to us all" or "You have a way with colors that makes a room comfortable

> *Being acknowledged helps people to flourish and thrive, and it inspires them to do even more.*

and inviting." Do you see the difference? Which one would you rather receive?

People love to be acknowledged because it's all about them and who they are. Being acknowledged helps people to flourish and thrive, and it inspires them to do even more. Acknowledging others is powerful. You're letting people see their greatness in the words you've chosen to describe them. You are supporting them to live success…from the inside out.

Begin to practice this advanced style of relating today. Consciously and sincerely acknowledge two people each day at work or at home. Do this for the next seven days or until it becomes a habit. It only takes seconds, yet its impact is timeless. Make their day and yours too, by acknowledging others often.

"A career is a job that has gone on too long."

—JEFF MCNELLY

27

TELL-TALE CLUES TO BEING OUT OF ALIGNMENT AT WORK

PEOPLE ARE HAPPIEST AND MOST PROSPEROUS in their work when it is aligned with what is meaningful to them and what they're passionate about. We happen to live in a rapidly changing work environment. What was joyful work one day can become dreaded work the next.

When things change, you want to make sure the changes are in alignment with what's most important to you—such as your values and your talents. If they're not, see if there are ways to bring them back into alignment. If it becomes clear that there are no ways to do that, then it's time to move on.

How can you tell if the changes are out of alignment for you? If you're in tune with yourself, your gut instincts or intuition will kick in with an answer. You can also talk to a trusted friend, family member, or mentor. Watch for these tell-tale clues: frustration, anger, fatigue,

> *You will be most happy and prosperous in your work when it is aligned with your values and talents.*

stress, boredom, taking things out on those close to you, being told you're no longer fun to be with.

The mistake many people make—when things stay out of alignment with what's most important to them—is to hang on too long to a job that no longer works for them. They end up settling for less because it's easier and safer. They don't want to take the risk or make the time to look for work that would be more joyful. Hanging on too long will result in the loss of self-respect, loss of self-confidence, and unhappiness. Don't let this happen to you.

Success…from the inside out means taking time to reflect on your current work. Ask yourself these questions:

- Am I passionate about what I'm doing?
- Am I using my talents and strengths?
- Am I happy in my work?
- Does it bring me joy and fulfillment?
- Am I earning what I deserve?

Remember: *people are happiest and most prosperous in their work when it is aligned with what is meaningful to them and what they're passionate about. That means you, too.*

*"Nurture your mind with your thoughts,
for you will never go any higher
than you think."*

—BENJAMIN DISRAELI

28

AN INSIDER'S VIEW TO "WHAT YOU FOCUS ON GETS BIGGER"

HAVE YOU NOTICED HOW MUCH EASIER IT IS to give words of wisdom and advice to other people rather than follow them for yourself? Well, that's what happened to me recently. Talk about a lesson learned.

I wanted to write an article about "what you focus on gets bigger." You've heard similar phrases like, "It's a self-fulfilling prophecy," "As it is within, so it is without," "What you think about, comes about," and "Where you put your attention, happens."

All I could think about was how I couldn't come up with the article for my upcoming newsletter. I couldn't think of how to write what I wanted to say. Inspiration was definitely not coming through. This was growing into a much harder topic than I thought it would be. I kept putting it off, finding everything else under the sun to do rather than writing. I ended up thinking that I better throw out this topic fast

> *What you think about, comes about. As it is within, so it is without. What you focus on, is exactly what you'll get.*

and come up with another one or else there wouldn't be any article this particular week.

And then in a flash, it hit me. What I was focusing on was getting bigger. I was creating exactly what I was thinking about. I was thinking about struggle and no article. Here I wanted to give you examples from some of my clients, and the best example that I could give you was my very own. The irony of it all made me laugh. The joke definitely was on me.

With that flash of insight, my perspective changed. What took me almost a week to do, suddenly came together very quickly. All it took was the right focus. And, the lesson I learned was that "what you focus on gets bigger" is very neutral. It doesn't care whether you're focusing on something negative or positive. Whatever it is, that's exactly what you'll get.

As you can see, thoughts can be very sneaky. Just when you think you're thinking positive thoughts, you find they're actually negative. Success…from the inside out means giving yourself empowering messages regularly so you can stay on track. Keeping these messages written down and in front of you is best. Sticky notes on a computer or refrigerator work great. And your message for this week is? You got it. "What you focus on gets bigger."

"The significant problems we have cannot be solved at the same level of thinking that created them."

—ALBERT EINSTEIN

29

REST IN SOLUTIONS
A Creative Approach To Problem-Solving

HOW OFTEN DO YOU CATCH YOURSELF dwelling on problems? How often do you notice others dwelling on problems? Are you even aware there is "dwelling" going on?

Dwelling on problems is a time waster and an energy drainer. It's also a habit. And it's definitely NOT the way to live success…from the inside out.

Can you remember a recent problem, either at work or at home, where everyone kept going around and around in circles and nothing got resolved? When you dwell on the problem, you are ineffective and non-productive. Certainly it's important for you to recognize when there's a problem and what caused it. Yet by going over and over the details, you bog yourself down. Keeping your attention on the problem is like crawling through the muck to get to the other side. You will eventually get there, yet it will be with great effort and frustration.

There is a better way. It's a concept called "resting in solutions." When you shift to resting in solutions, you tap into your creative

> *Rise above the muck of the problem and rest in the multitude of possible solutions.*

thinking and begin to brainstorm. Your attention is put on all the possible solutions you can think of. By resting in these solutions—the possibilities—the best one will reveal itself to you so you can take positive action.

Resting in solutions generates a velocity and a momentum that energizes you to get your creative juices flowing. It's a catalyst to propel you above and beyond the problem into the realm of possibilities and creative solutions. This works in all situations—at home, at work, in life. And it works no matter what your role—boss, parent, friend, partner, spouse, or colleague. When you rest in solutions, you put your focus directly on creativity, possibilities, and results.

Notice where you're putting your attention. Is it on the problem or the solution? Catch yourself when you find you're dwelling on the problem. Immediately shift gears to rest in the solutions. Get creative. Engage others to play with you. Choose a problem that you've been dwelling on and start to brainstorm possible solutions right now. Watch for the best one to surface and then act on it.

Did you know that there are up to 25 different ways to solve a problem? It's true! So, I challenge you to get out of the muck of the problem and empower yourself to play in the multitude of possible solutions. Make your mantra this week "rest in solutions."

"Life cannot be hurried."

—MAASAI SAYING

30

THE JOY OF MOSEYING, MAYBERRY STYLE

HERE'S A BLAST FROM THE PAST. Do you remember *The Andy Griffith Show*? You know—Andy, Opie, Aunt Bea, Barney, Mayberry. They sure had the joy of moseying down pat. No "hurry sickness" evident in that town. They knew how to move at a leisurely pace: meandering out to Miller's Pond, strolling over to Floyd's barbershop, sauntering by the old courthouse, enjoying Aunt Bea's meals without haste, slow moving traffic down main street. They were a happy bunch. Their secret was mastering the joy of moseying.

I know television is not real life. Yet, Mayberry is such a great illustration of moseying. Moseying is very much lacking in our current lifestyles. It's close to becoming extinct, having been replaced with the "hurry sickness." Hurry here. Hurry there. Rush. Rush. Rush. The Hurry Sickness 10K Run is filled daily with willing participants.

> *Take a lesson from Andy, Opie, Aunt Bea, and Barney. Do the Mayberry Mosey!*

Maybe you run that race every day. It's really becoming an epidemic. And what's the prize if you win the race? You get to hurry even more! It sounds exhausting, doesn't it? So, what's the cure for the "hurry sickness?" A good dose of moseying.

Deciding whether or not to mosey is entirely up to you. It takes courage to step out of the human "race." You can start by slowing down. Walk slower. Speak slower. Drive slower. Eat slower. Relish each moment rather than thinking about what's next. Take your time. Move at a leisurely pace. Turn off your pagers and cell phones. Stop and smell the roses. You'll notice a difference in how you feel just by doing these few things.

When you take the time to mosey and slow down, you'll find that it will positively impact your effectiveness and productivity at work, not to mention being nicer to the people close to you.

How about it? Do you want to slow down? Are you ready to start moseying? Perhaps you're saying that there is no way you can fit this into your life. It's just not possible. Well, how about committing to moseying for just one day? Go ahead. Give it a try. You can mosey for one day. You may even decide you like doing this so much that you'll end up moseying on a regular basis.

This week put your "hurry sickness" aside and bring the joy of moseying back into your life. Take a lesson from Andy, Opie, Aunt Bea, and Barney. Do the Mayberry Mosey!

*"Speak clearly, if you speak at all;
carve every word before you let it fall."*

—OLIVER WENDELL HOLMES

31

A SURE-FIRE WAY TO QUICKLY IMPROVE HOW YOU COMMUNICATE

THE WORDS YOU CHOOSE IN COMMUNICATING with others make a big difference in how well you connect with the people in your life. Just a few simple words can either build bridges or build walls. Bridges keep the communication flowing easily and harmoniously. Walls create distance and cause disharmony. Which do you want to build? If you want to live success…from the inside out, make sure you're building bridges.

How often do you find yourself using these words "should" and "have to?" What effect do they have on the people you're talking to? Do they seem to shut down, get defensive, or become angry? Do you also use these words with yourself? What happens to you when you find yourself being "shoulded" or "have to'd?"

Let's say someone says to you, "You *should* do that." "You *have* to get this done right now." Your thoughts might be, "DON'T tell me

> *Just a few simple words can make all the difference between building bridges or building walls.*

what to do." "No way, buster." "Should" and "have to" have a feeling of judgment or authority attached to them. They cause a negative reaction. These words build walls.

To make them into bridge builders you might say, "Consider trying it this way." "When do you think you might be able to get this done?" There's a definite difference in the energy around these words. Can you feel it? It's these bridge-building words that help to keep the communication flowing in a positive direction.

Not long ago, a colleague heard me talk about "should" and "have to." She started noticing when these words popped up in conversation. She told me about becoming aware of how she felt when people (especially her husband) spoke to her using "should" and "have to." She didn't like it. And, she realized she was a user of these words too. Needless to say, she has become much more conscious of the words she chooses.

Remember, a sure-fire way to quickly improve your all-around communication is to immediately eliminate "should" and "have to" from your language. Become aware of when you use these words with yourself and others. Notice the reactions to them. Be aware of people using these words with you and how you react to them.

To create harmonious communication, make sure the words you choose build bridges rather than build walls. Stop "shoulding" and "have to-ing" on yourself and others. Begin building bridges today, and hit delete on "should" and "have to!"

"I finally figured out that the reason to be alive is to enjoy it."

—RITA MAE BROWN

32

TWELVE WAYS TO TAKE MINI-SPRING BREAKS... ALL YEAR LONG!

SPRING BREAK! FUN IN THE SUN. Food and beverages. Friends and romance. Rest and relaxation. Laughter, connection, get-away. It's that time of the year which college students look forward to for months...their annual trek South. And, how about you? What have you been looking forward to?

Recently, a client shared with me how overwhelmed, frustrated, and burned-out she was feeling. She is a small business owner working long hours. In addition, she has a leadership position with a volunteer non-profit organization that takes up much of her free time. Day after day, she's working and helping others. There's no time for herself. When I asked her what she had to look forward to each week, she had trouble thinking of something. It's no wonder she's feeling the way she is. She's not having any fun.

Just like setting time aside for meetings and work projects, it's important to set time aside just for you. This time can be spent alone or with others you enjoy. It can last 15 minutes, a few hours, or all day.

> *Mini-spring breaks feed your soul, rejuvenate your body, and clear your mind. They are a vital ingredient to living success…from the inside out.*

You are actually scheduling a mini-spring break that you can look forward to every single week. Not sure what to do? Here's a 5-minute exercise (which I've adapted from an exercise in Julia Cameron's book, *The Artist's Way*) to give you some ideas:

1. Make a list of 12 things you have enjoyed doing. (Gardening, going to a movie, cooking, dancing, giving and getting a massage, biking, playing games, reading, bowling, symphony, attending a ball game, hiking, etc.)
2. Go back over your list and date the last time you did each one.
3. Are you surprised to find that it's been months or even years since you've done some of the things you enjoy?

You now have 12 weeks of something to look forward to each week. These mini-spring breaks allow the playful part of you to come out. They feed your soul, rejuvenate your body, and clear your mind. Plus, they help you to be more productive and efficient at work. Mini-spring breaks are important to your overall well-being. They are a vital ingredient to living success…from the inside out.

Commit to having something fun to look forward to for the next 12 weeks. Get started right now and choose one favorite thing from your list above. Make this your mini-spring break for the week and schedule it into your calendar. Then choose another favorite from your list and make it your mini-spring break for the next week, and so on. After the end of your 12 weeks, repeat the process.

Make it a habit to take mini-spring breaks all year long. Relax, laugh, connect, and play. Be like a college student—it's party time.

*"Pleasant words are a honeycomb,
sweet to the soul
and healing to the bones."*

—PROVERBS 16:24

33

THE ART OF APPRECIATING SUCCESS

CULTIVATING THE ART OF APPRECIATING SUCCESS is one of the most valuable things you can do. Unfortunately, it's become a lost art in our society. Most of us move at such a fast pace that we don't take time out to say thank you or give praise to each other. And, we neglect doing the same for ourselves, too.

We are way under-appreciated and under-acknowledged in our culture. It's a condition that runs rampant in the workplace and even in our homes. And, the place where it's most at risk is in how we treat ourselves. How often do you appreciate your own successes and acknowledge your own accomplishments? How often do you pat yourself on the back for a job well done? Chances are not very often because you've been programmed to focus on what didn't work rather than what did.

A small business client found that a little appreciation on his part had a huge impact on his employees. His two assistants had been working very hard and complaining about being overwhelmed. It

> *Remember to take time out daily to say thank you and give praise to others and yourself.*

occurred to him that perhaps it wasn't so much a matter of being overwhelmed, but more a matter of being under-appreciated. He certainly knew he was guilty of giving out more criticism than praise. So, he told them he wanted to take them out to lunch to show his appreciation; they were thrilled.

On the day of the lunch he was surprised when one of the women (who always wore casual clothes to work) came in wearing a dress and make-up. He then realized how important this lunch was to her and how a little appreciation goes a long way. He also noticed in the days afterwards that his assistants were happier and not complaining. What changed? The workload was the same. The difference was that they felt appreciated and acknowledged for the work they were doing. Think about it. What builds self-confidence? What generates enthusiasm and motivation? Is it criticism or praise? I'm sure you'll agree with me: the answer is praise.

People who live success…from the inside out make it a regular practice to cultivate the art of appreciating success. They recognize that appreciating successes, acknowledging accomplishments, and rewarding achievement balances out the negative, builds self-confidence, and boosts spirits. Ultimately, the art of appreciating success generates more success.

You can begin to appreciate more of your successes, and those of others, by shifting your focus from what's not working to what is working. Start with appreciating 5 people tomorrow by saying thank you and giving praise. Then, appreciate yourself by making a list of your 5 successes for the day. Just by writing them down, you're acknowledging your accomplishments.

With a few kind words and some simple gestures, you'll be well on your way to cultivating the art of appreciating success. By doing so, smiles will abound for both you and the people you appreciate. Thank you for doing your part to actively bring back this lost art—you are appreciated!

"If you wait until the wind and the weather are just right, you will never plant anything and never harvest anything."

—ECCLESIASTES 11:4

34

COMMON CHARACTERISTICS OF THE PERFECTLY PERFECT

D O YOU STRIVE TO BE A PERFECT PATTY or a Perfect Patrick? Do you spend hours trying to make a project at work or at home just right? Do you worry that what you're doing or saying won't be good enough? Do you procrastinate on getting started, stop in the middle, or just not finish?

These are just some of the characteristics of a perfectionist. Maybe you see some of these characteristics in yourself and are saying, "Yes, that's me." Being a perfectionist puts lots of strain, pressure, and stress on yourself. If you are prone to these tendencies, ask yourself whose standards you're trying to live up to: yours or someone else's.

The *American Heritage* definition of perfectionism is "a propensity for setting extremely high standards and being displeased with any-

> *Rather than trying to please others, please yourself instead—by doing your best and knowing it's good enough.*

thing less." My definition of perfectionism is driving yourself and others crazy.

It's not necessary to stress yourself by constantly trying to live up to a level of unattainable perfectionism. I'm sure this is something you wouldn't wish on others, so why would you wish it on yourself? If you want to live success…from the inside out, then it's time to give up perfectionism.

Yes, you want to do your best. Yes, you want to be known for doing a good job. No, it doesn't have to be "perfectly perfect." What is perfect to you may not be perfect to someone else anyway. Rather than trying to please others, please yourself instead by doing your best and knowing it's good enough.

Give yourself a break this week. Relieve the pressure you've been putting on yourself. Begin to hold yourself to a new standard: the standard of striving for excellence, rather than striving for perfect perfection. I promise you that it will make your life much easier, and you'll be happier with the results.

Practice letting go of having to be "perfectly perfect" about something right now. Make your new mantra "strive for excellence, rather than perfection." Post this mantra as a reminder wherever you will see it—on your computer, mirror, refrigerator, calendar, and telephone. You'll thank yourself for it.

"If you don't make time to take care of yourself, who will?"

—CONNIE PODESTA

35

A PERSONALIZED STRATEGY FOR PUTTING YOURSELF FIRST

THIS WEEK A CLIENT E-MAILED ME saying she'd like to skip her coaching session as she was very pre-occupied with her mother's illness. She felt she wouldn't be focused enough to be effective during our coaching time. Our tendency, when we are thrust into a caretaking role, is to give our all to those people in need. Whether they are ailing parents, young children, a demanding boss, a stressed out co-worker, a needy friend, or a spouse who wants more time, it's natural to want to put them first above our own needs. Yet when we consistently do this over time, we will suffer…and so will they.

You may think this doesn't apply to you. However, if you're feeling stressed, overwhelmed, frustrated, or fatigued, ask yourself if you are constantly putting the needs of others before your own. If yes, then eventually your feelings will be sensed by—and taken out on—

> *Your greatest gift to those you care about is to take care of yourself first.*

those very people you are trying to help. This is not a win-win situation by any means.

When too much of your time and energy is extended towards others, it will be at the expense of your own self-care. People often say, "It's selfish to put myself first. I can't do that. What will people think of me?" We've been taught from an early age that it's wrong to be selfish. But I'm not talking about being selfish in a negative way. I'm talking about putting yourself first as a form of self-care. When you do this, you'll be in a much better place—physically, mentally, and emotionally—to be fully available for the important people in your life. Your greatest gift to them is to take care of yourself first.

Ask yourself these questions:

- What does putting myself first mean to me?
- Where am I not putting myself first?
- How have I been letting my self-care slip?
- What three things can I do right now to begin practicing self-care?
- What three activities can I eliminate from my week so I have more time for me?

Here are some ideas to get you started: say no to requests, go to bed earlier, make that doctor's appointment, do something fun each day, let go of a volunteer activity, stop staying late at work, hire a housekeeper. By practicing self-care, you increase your capacity to live success…from the inside out. It might seem awkward at first to put this kind of focus just on you; give yourself permission to do so anyway. You deserve to start putting yourself first.

*"In life we cannot avoid change,
we cannot avoid loss.
Freedom and happiness are found
in the flexibility and ease with which we
move through change."*

—BUDDHA

36

EASE YOUR WAY THROUGH CAREER CHANGE
An Emotional Survival Kit

GOING THROUGH CAREER CHANGE, or being part of a company-initiated restructuring, can be a big blow to your nervous system. There are many resources out there to help you with a job search. Yet, what about the emotional side of change? Our emotions often take a back seat to finding that new job. And, it's our emotions that are vital to living success…from the inside out. The following is an emotional survival kit filled with three tools to help navigate you through this transition. They've proven to be valuable to many of my clients, and my wish is that they'll be helpful for you, too.

> *Acknowledge your emotions. Monitor your thoughts. Be open to possibilities.*

1. Acknowledge Your Emotions

Change of any kind stirs up all kinds of emotions, whether it's change you've chosen or change that's been forced upon you. It's important to acknowledge the emotions, feel them, and release them. If you don't, the emotions will hold you back. Ignoring them doesn't mean they'll go away. What you hide from will run you. And dwelling on the emotions will keep you stuck. Give emotions the importance they deserve. Talk to a trusted friend. Write about your feelings. Cry. Get angry. Feel the fear. Do something physical to release them. Unresolved anger at a boss or a company will come through in an interview (no matter how much you think you're hiding it) if you haven't come to terms with it.

2. Monitor Your Thoughts

What you focus on gets bigger. If you have negative thoughts, then you'll get negative results. If you have positive thoughts, then you'll get positive results. Keep a sharp look out on your thoughts and self-talk. Thinking "No one will hire me at my age" will not move you on to success. Thinking "They are fortunate to hire me with all my wisdom and experience," will. Thoughts are a self-fulfilling prophecy. Make sure you maintain a positive mental environment and come from a positive attitude. Reframe those negative thoughts into positive ones.

3. Consider the Possibilities

Deciding to make a career change, or being restructured out of your job, may be just the break you're looking for to try something new.

Get together with your friends or family. Brainstorm all the possibilities that are now opening up to you such as starting a home-based business, temporary or part-time work, changing careers, going back to school, contract work, taking time off to be with family, traveling, turning a hobby into a business, and so on. Get outrageous. Be excited. The sky's the limit.

It's vital that you continuously acknowledge your emotions and monitor your thoughts so you can be fully open to consider the possibilities. This is an on-going process and will require a sincere commitment on your part. If you let your heavy emotions and negative thoughts camp out rent-free in your consciousness, then you won't have the space available for the possibilities to shine through. Use this emotional survival kit to ease your way through career change.

"Everyone has been made for some particular work and the desire for that work has been put in their hearts."

—RUMI

37

MORE TOOLS TO EASE YOUR WAY THROUGH CAREER CHANGE

Now that you've learned how your emotional survival kit can help you, it's time to apply the "practical" tools. These three tools complement your emotional survival kit to help you move into your new career as quickly and as easily as possible.

1. Take Stock of Your Finances

One reason why people fear career change is because they think they'll make less than they're currently earning. They're afraid the bills won't get paid. Most often this fear isn't grounded in reality. Stay out of this fear trap and take time to find out exactly where your money is going. Identify your monthly expenses. Determine what you have in savings and investments. Eliminate unnecessary expenses. Ask for financial help if you need it.

> *Expert advice is often just what you need to get you where you want to go more quickly and easily—and with less stress.*

Knowledge brings with it peace of mind. Find out exactly what you have, what you'll need, and how or where to get it. Then you'll be in a better position to know your salary's bottom line when you go to look for a new job. Sometimes, if you make a complete career transition, you may start at a lower income; however, that will change as you gain experience. And of course, there's always this option: you could find new work, whether it's in your current field or a different one, and receive a higher income! This happens often. Your experience and transferable skills are worth a lot in the marketplace.

2. Use Available Resources
There are many different resources available to you in your career search. They can be in the form of skills training for resume writing, interviewing techniques, and salary negotiation. They can also be employee assistance programs, career planning workshops, and on-line career programs. Make sure you take advantage of all these resources. They are there to help you make as smooth a career transition as possible.

Many of these services are free or reasonably priced. You can find them at the local community college, in the career office at the university you attended, in books at the bookstore, in job assistance programs at area churches, and on the Internet as on-line courses. Also, you'll find private enterprises and career professionals who specialize in offering career services. Ask your friends if they've used any of these services, and ask for a referral.

3. Get Expert Help

You don't need to carry the load all by yourself. And, loved ones can be limited in the counsel they give. Expert and objective assistance is often just the catalyst you need to get you where you want to go more quickly and easily—and with less stress. Not sure how to make a wise career change? Hire a career coach. Getting bogged down in the emotions? Go to a therapist. Can't figure out your finances? See a financial planner.

Let these three practical tools and your emotional survival kit act as your dynamic duo as you ease your way through career change. And, may I be the first to congratulate you on your new career!

"The wind and the waves are always on the side of the ablest navigators."

—EDWARD GIBBONS

38

SIX STEPS TO A SMOOTH RE-ENTRY

ID YOU TAKE A "SUMMER BREAK" from a regular activity, ease up on your sales prospecting, put half-finished projects on the back burner, or lose track of friends or colleagues? If yes, then now is the time to come back to the real world, back to "school" so to speak. It's time to re-enter the atmosphere from which you've been away. Will yours be a bumpy ride or a smooth re-entry?

Recently, I was a guest at an Optimist's Club luncheon. A sales professional asked me how he could get back into the swing of prospecting and generating new sales. He was having trouble getting motivated to take action. His was a timely question as I was wondering the same thing for myself about returning to the rhythm of my writing. I realized after pondering his question that re-entry takes more than a "just do it" answer.

> *The essence of what you desire is where true motivation lies; it's your touchstone.*

A 6-STEP PROCESS TO HELP YOUR RE-ENTRY BE A SMOOTH RIDE

1. Desire

Define the essence of what re-entry will bring you. More time, money, connection, love, well-being, success, fulfillment, fun, peace of mind. That's where the motivation lies: your touchstone. If it's not your heart's desire, if someone's "shoulding" on you, then drop it. Or, refine it until it is.

2. Intention

State out loud, or write down, what it is you want. This is the intention you're sending out to the Universe. The Universe will then meet you half way to help you co-create the results. Your Higher Power is always ready to assist you whenever you are clear and sincere.

3. Commitment

Pledge to yourself that you will do whatever it takes to make this smooth re-entry happen.

4. Support:

It's not necessary to do it all alone. Support comes from three places: internal strength, other people, and a Higher Power. Decide which systems will best support you. Set up an accountability check-in system with select friends or colleagues. Hire a coach. Pray. Meditate. Take time for yourself.

5. Action

Identify the action steps you need to take. Run them by someone else for a reality check. Re-commit to taking the actions necessary for a smooth re-entry and then do whatever it takes to make that happen.

6. Fine-Tune

Re-entry may require some adjustments along the way. You know what you're capable of. Stretch at first to get started. If it's right, you'll be in the flow. If there are some bumps, you'll fine-tune it by making the changes needed for a smooth ride.

Notice that "action" is the fifth step rather than the first. Many people "just do it" without any reflection, then hit bumpy terrain and wonder why they falter or stop. Taking time to do the first four steps will set your environment up for success…from the inside out. It's your foundation that will ensure the meaningful action steps for you to take. It's your key to achieving a smooth re-entry rather than a bumpy ride.

Decide today where you want to engage in re-entry. Take time this week to set up your environment for success. Go through each of the first 4 steps in the re-entry process. This won't take long. Then and only then, do steps 5 and 6. Now you're back in the swing of things. Reap the results of your actions and enjoy a smooth re-entry.

*"Alone we can do so little.
Together we can do so much."*

—HELEN KELLER

39

THREE SOURCES OF SUPPORT FOR SUCCESS-MINDED PEOPLE

༄

SUCCESS-MINDED PEOPLE KNOW that their success is a team effort. It takes much more than just individual effort to create or achieve something great. Sure you can be successful on your own; yet when you bring others into the picture, a synergy begins to build, and you end up with something greater than if you had done it all on your own.

You may be thinking that the members of the team I'm referring to includes you and the people you work or live with. However, they are just a small part of the whole. I'm suggesting you bring in the added dimension of sources greater than yourself who will lift you up to heights you couldn't possibly reach without them. This high-level support comes from three places:

> *When you join forces with others, a synergy builds and you end up with something greater than if you had done it on your own.*

1. Your Inner Self
This is the higher part of you, the wisdom part, and is the seat of your intuition. It's your inner compass always guiding you to what's best for you. This is your still small voice within. Many people don't consider their inner self as an integral part of their success and consequently only look to the outer self they show to the world. Embrace the support of your inner self. Listen to and follow what it has to say, as it holds all the answers and knows what's right for you.

2. The Angels Next Door
Your angels next door are those people who impact you in significant and profound ways. And, they usually aren't your family or friends. That's not to say your family, friends, and colleagues don't influence you positively. What I'm talking about are the angels outside that circle. They can be a mentor, coach, minister, or teacher. These are the people who encourage you to take the road less traveled, who embolden you to stretch to reach your full potential. When the angels next door appear on your doorstep, allow them to help you as their support and influence can change the course of your life.

3. A Higher Power
There is a Higher Power who has a much bigger plan for you than you can ever begin to imagine. Instead of trying to control things, turn

them over to your Higher Power through prayer and meditation. Ask for guidance and assistance. You may receive what you asked for, or you may receive something even greater that looks completely different. Whenever you surrender to your Higher Power, you can be sure that you will be supported in ways that are only for your highest good.

Decide today to give up the "I can do it on my own" thinking and do what other people who live success…from the inside out do: let your success be a team effort. Join forces with your higher self, the angels next door, and your Higher Power and watch your success soar to realms you couldn't reach on your own. Allow the synergy of this high-powered, high-level support team to become a regular part of your life. When you do, you'll wonder how you ever got along without them.

"No one can make you feel inferior without your consent."

—ELEANOR ROOSEVELT

40

FIVE STEPS TO BEATING THE COMPARISON BLUES

TO COMPARE OR NOT TO COMPARE, that is the question. Does any of this sound familiar to you? You look at someone's achievements and all of a sudden you feel like you should be doing more. Your partner is in fabulous shape. You take a look at yourself and instantly feel like flab city. You're in a conversation with colleagues and before you know it, you're feeling like a mental midget. If you answered yes to any of these (or to something similar), then you've been hit with the comparison blues.

Watch out for the comparison blues. They sneak up on you without warning. One minute you're on top of the world, and the next minute you're in the pits. You don't even know what hit you. All you know is that you are now down in the dumps, and it feels crummy.

> *You are unique, unlike anyone else on this earth, with your own special talents and gifts.*

Don't despair. It happens to everyone. And, there is an antidote.

The comparison blues is a space you move into when you've been comparing yourself to someone else. It's a place where you feel less than adequate, where you wallow in misery, where you beat yourself up. This is not a pleasant place to be. And, it's a block to living

SUCCESS...FROM THE INSIDE OUT!

I know all about the comparison blues. They hit me not long ago when another coach and I were co-facilitating a train-the-coach program. On the third day of the training, I was watching my colleague do her thing and marveled at her brilliance as a facilitator. All of a sudden, I went into instant intimidation and felt very inadequate. How could I possibly follow her? She was so good. I really began to doubt my own capabilities as a trainer and facilitator.

Now bear in mind that I didn't have any problem with this on Day One or Day Two. Fortunately, I realized I was being hit right between the eyes with the comparison blues. I reminded myself of my talents and the unique abilities and style I was bringing to the trainer team. With that awareness, I went on to finish Day Three with a flourish.

Don't let the comparison blues block you from your success. Don't let it keep you captive either. If you find yourself in the clutches of the comparison blues, quickly take the following "Comparison Blues Antidote:"

1. Be aware that you're comparing yourself to someone else.
2. Acknowledge that you are unique with your own special talents and gifts.
3. Ask yourself if there is something about the other person you'd honestly like for yourself.
4. If so, decide what small action you can take to start getting you there and do it right away.
5. If the comparison blues persist, do a reality check. Talk to a supportive friend, mentor, or coach who can quickly point you back to reality.

How do you know when you've been hit with the comparison blues? The biggest clue is when you find yourself feeling inadequate—all of a sudden. Chances are good that you're comparing yourself to someone else. Catch yourself as soon as you can. Immediately take the comparison blues antidote and stop singing the comparison blues.

"Freedom lies in being bold."

—ROBERT FROST

41

TEN SECONDS OF BOLDNESS, TWICE A DAY

J UST AS BRUSHING YOUR TEETH TWICE A DAY IS A HABIT and a discipline, so is practicing ten seconds of boldness, twice a day. Ten seconds of boldness, twice a day is a call to action to say and do whatever takes courage to say and do. And, it's something that people who live success…from the inside out practice every day.

Ten seconds of boldness, twice a day has to do with the courage to ask for what you want. The courage to pick up the phone to make that call. The courage to say what's hard to say. The courage to ask for the sale or the raise. The courage to step out of your comfort zone.

If you stay in your comfort zone, you'll achieve ho-hum success. If you take too big of a leap, you'll land in the panic zone of chaos, fear, anxiety, and most likely failure. Ten seconds of boldness, twice a day takes you into that "can-do" zone between comfort and panic. It takes you into the stretch zone where there is no complacency or craziness, and where you are emboldened to achieve results in a way that feels doable, exciting, and fun in bite-size manageable pieces.

The reason you do this twice a day is similar to riding a horse. If you fall off the horse, what happens? You get back up on the horse.

> *Answer the call to action to say and do whatever takes courage to say and do.*

Well, the same holds true here. If you don't achieve the results you want with your first ten seconds of boldness, you get right back up on the horse by exercising another. And chances are, you'll have success the second time around.

Here's an example of ten seconds of boldness:

A year ago, a fellow coach talked with a non-profit executive about coaching him and his staff of 25. It was a huge organizational development project, and she felt she wasn't ready for it yet. So consequently, she never followed-up.

A year later, she felt ready. But she wasn't sure if the executive would remember her. After spending 20 minutes trying to talk herself into calling him, she decided to just do it and see where it led. Her ten seconds of boldness came with that decision to pick up the phone. It turns out he did remember their conversation and was ready to begin the coaching program right there on the spot.

What are your two ten seconds of boldness going to be today? Are you ready to courageously move into the stretch zone to achieve the success you want? If yes, then let today be the first day of a new daily discipline. Put this short, memorable, and powerful call to action on sticky notes everywhere as your constant reminders to make it a habit to practice: "ten seconds of boldness, twice a day." Just do it!

"Faith is believing in things when common sense says not to."

—GEORGE SEATON

42

LISTEN TO
THE MESSAGES

NEVER UNDERESTIMATE THE POWER of the Universe. It is constantly talking to you and sending you messages. The question is, "Are you paying attention and listening to the messages?" If you're like most people, you're usually not because your radar screen is focused on your own agenda and that of others.

A client came to me to help her move into a new line of work. She had five career options to pursue, yet she was overlooking one thing—photography. She already had her hand in it part-time, and she was an excellent photographer. But because it brought her so much joy and because it felt like play, she didn't think being a photographer qualified as a viable and respectable form of employment for her. Plus, she felt she couldn't make a living at it.

So, she kept looking at her other options such as sales, real estate, financial positions, and non-profit work—being convinced that they were the best ways for her to go.

As time went on, an interesting thing began to happen. First of all, none of the above options were panning out. Secondly, photography jobs began to show up out of the blue. She wasn't even pursuing them,

52 WAYS TO LIVE SUCCESS...

> *The Universe has a much easier way for you, and its desire is to take you the quickest way possible to what's best for you.*

and these opportunities were literally dropping out of the sky into her lap. Then another photographer saw her work, was very impressed, and wanted to partner up with her to do specialty wedding photography—just the kind of work she really enjoyed. And last but not least, quite unexpectedly, her relatives gave her an expensive piece of photography equipment for Christmas.

The Universe was sending my client very clear messages that were guiding her to her new career. They were becoming so obvious that she could no longer avoid them. Her comment was, "The Universe keeps sending me in the photography direction. I think I'll pursue this." Bingo! Her radar screen finally cleared up so she could see the messages that were being sent. With that, she decided to go with the flow and is now in the process of building a fun, lucrative, and successful photography business.

I tell you this story because the Universe is sending messages to you, too. These messages will be unique to your situation and will guide you to what you're to do and the direction you're to go. If you want to live success...from the inside out, let these messages be the information you use in making your decisions.

The Universe has an easier way for you, and its desire is to take you the quickest way possible to what's best for you. Unfortunately, when you don't listen to the messages, you often choose what turns out to be a harder and longer way. So, why not make it easy on yourself and start paying attention when the Universe speaks to you?

Remember: never underestimate the power of the Universe. Listen to the messages.

"A smile is the lighting system of the face and the heating system of the heart."

—BARBARA JOHNSON

43

THE IMPORTANCE OF A SMILE

~~~~~~~~

"SMILE, AND THE WORLD SMILES WITH YOU." Doesn't it feel great when people smile at you? Doesn't it make you want to smile right back? (Well okay, most of the time you do.) What would it be like if you were no longer able to smile? How would that impact you and the people you interact with at work and in life?

Today I had lunch with a remarkable lady. Carol and I have been friends for the last seven years and as she shared with me her story of the past year, I was in awe of how her inner strength and human spirit have helped her survive and continue to survive a very difficult experience. Carol is definitely a shining example of a person living success…from the inside out.

This past year has been most challenging for my friend. She had a life-threatening illness and almost died on the surgeon's table. On top of that, she awoke with one side of her face paralyzed. Now that would be devastating to most people, but it's even more so for Carol because she makes her livelihood as a professional speaker.

> *A smile is an expression of you from your heart.*

What touched me so deeply was how troubling it was for Carol not to be able to smile anymore. I could tell it was a great loss for her. Thank goodness that with continued therapy her paralysis will go away, and she'll be able to smile again. In the meantime, it's agony.

A smile seems to be such a simple thing and yet it wasn't until I talked with Carol that I realized how important it is, and just how much I've taken it for granted.

A smile is an expression of you from your heart. It's a way of instantly connecting with others and expressing joy, warmth, and caring. It's a gift you give without thinking. Imagine having that gift taken away from you. Imagine not being able to smile at your child, spouse, parent, client, co-worker, customer, or friend. What would that be like for you? How important is your smile to you now?

Carol's smile was taken away by outside circumstances. Your smile is only taken away by you. You have the ability to smile at will. Yet, how often do you withhold it because you're walking around with a frown on your face, glaring at people, or just not seeing people, because you're so frazzled and busy? How does not smiling affect your interactions at work and in life?

Your smile IS important. When you recognize that it's more than just a simple smile, when you give it away freely because you can, it will uplift both you and the people you're smiling at.

Practice living success…from the inside out every day by appreciating the importance of a smile. With every smile you freely give, may it take Carol one smile closer to regaining her own. Remember: smile, and the world smiles with you. What simpler or greater gift is there?

*"Striving for excellence
is stimulating and rewarding.
Striving for perfection
is both obsessive and futile."*

—EDWIN C. BLISS

44

HOW TO OVERCOME PERFECTIONISM AND PROCRASTINATION

∼∾∽

WHENEVER WE WORK ON SOMETHING important, we want things to be just right. We want to do it perfectly. We want someone to say, "You did a great job."

This desire to be perfect can get in your way. It can take you into thoughts of fear such as, "I'm afraid if I don't do it perfectly, then I'll be a failure, I'll be criticized, I'll look stupid, or I'll succeed." Having to do things perfectly can cause you to get so bogged down that you end up procrastinating to the point where you never finish—or never start. As you can see, perfectionism and procrastination are closely related; and they hold you back from living success…from the inside out.

While I was working on a deadline for a writing project, I kept putting off the last third of my project. After days of resistance and avoiding my computer, I remembered a guideline I had put in place to keep me on track, "strive for excellence, not perfection." With that in mind, I decided to answer this statement in as many ways as I could

> *Strive for excellence, rather than perfection.*

to determine what was holding me back: "If I were to strive for excellence rather than perfection, I would…"

Some of my answers were, "I would write more quickly." "I would let go of trying to figure out the right words and write what's in my heart instead." "I would trust that my writing is inspiring and motivating just as it is." "I would write as if I'm speaking to someone."

When I asked myself, "Then why aren't I doing these things?" I found that I was afraid the third part of my project wouldn't be as good as the first two parts, and I really wanted it to be perfect because this was going to be read by many people. My fear was keeping me stuck and blocked. It was putting my project on hold until I could come up with the perfect words, which of course never came.

Once I saw this, I realized that no matter how perfect something is, there's always room for improvement. And the truth is that by striving for excellence, you'll end up with a much better result than you would if you were striving for perfection. What a revelation! After days of procrastination, I sat down and started writing with a greater sense of freedom and relief. What it took was a shift in thinking from perfection to excellence. And with that, my blocks and resistance fell away.

What are you trying to do perfectly? Where are you procrastinating? Identify one thing and answer this statement in as many ways as you can, "If I were to strive for excellence rather than perfection, I would…"

Next ask yourself, "Then why aren't I doing these things?" and see what fear-based answers show up for you. Just being aware of your fear will allow you to move forward. Decide what actions you want to take, and then handle what you want to accomplish with more confidence and ease. Go ahead. Give it a try. Start to overcome perfectionism and procrastination today.

> *"Do not let great ambitions overshadow small successes."*
>
> —CHINESE FORTUNE COOKIE

45

HOW TO RECOGNIZE SUCCESS IN "FAILURE"

**Where are you putting your focus?
Is it on success or on "failure?"**

A CLIENT I'M WORKING WITH SET A GOAL to enroll three pilot customers within 90 days for his new Internet business. Each week, he took the steps necessary to help him achieve his goal. And, each week he was one step closer to his accomplishment.

The end of his target was drawing near, and he still had two more customers to enroll. His deadline passed without achieving his goal. Even though he had many potential customers, there were some details he had to work out first, which he hadn't originally thought of. Therefore, in his mind, he decided he had failed in achieving his goal. He was very disappointed and became discouraged and de-motivat-

> *Successful people look at what's worked, learn from what hasn't, set new priorities, and then move on.*

ed. And consequently, he completely missed the success that was buried in his perceived "failure."

I suggested he take a look at Bill Gates. Certainly he had his share of "failures" along the way. When he failed to reach one of his goals, did he let that stop him? Absolutely not!

Gates re-evaluated the goal, re-grouped, and revised. And, you can bet he didn't do this all on his own. He asked his key people to help. Gates recognized that successful people look at what's worked, learn from what hasn't, set new priorities, and then move on. You don't see them dragging their "failures" into work with them every morning. Gates is where he is because he knows the importance of looking for the success in the "failure."

My client then put on his "Bill Gates" hat. He re-evaluated the goal he had set and realized that had it not been for the actions he had already taken, he wouldn't have known he had to first shore up his business infrastructure in order to be ready for his customers. What first looked like a failure was actually a success. Once he took the time to reflect on and recognize the success in his "failure," he was able to re-group and revise his strategy to reach his goal. He was now back on his way to achieving success…from the inside out.

It's important for you to see the process my client took so you can do the same. Ask yourself this, "Where are you focusing on failure rather than success?" Take one perceived "failure" and follow the steps below:

HOW TO RECOGNIZE SUCCESS IN "FAILURE," AN EXERCISE

A. Re-evaluate
1. Look at what worked well
2. Look at what didn't work well
3. Determine what you learned

B. Re-group and Revise
1. See the success and let go of the "failure"
2. Identify where to go next
3. Set new priorities
4. Revise your goal and do whatever it takes to get there

Whenever you feel like you've failed in something, put on your "Bill Gates" hat and look for the success in the "failure."

"Energy is the power that drives every human being."

—GERMAINE GREER

46

TWO WAYS TO SHIFT YOUR ENERGY

∞

YOU ARE RESPONSIBLE FOR BEING AWARE of your energy and for bringing it back into balance when it's out of balance. People often get stuck in their mental energy (thoughts and states of mind) and in their emotional energy (feelings). The fastest way to move that energy is by using your body.

Movement and breath are two powerful ways to shift your energy. They affect your nervous system to create positive change…from the inside out. Below are examples of how energy can become stuck, and ways for you to shift that energy:

1. Move Your Body

Sitting at your desk and working all day long creates tension in your body and mental fatigue. To move this energy, get up and stretch. Stamp your feet on the ground. Walk to your car and back. Swing your

> *Breathing deeply has a calming effect on your nervous system and brings you back into a balanced state.*

arms. Clap your hands. Walk or work out at lunch. Move your body in any way you want. You've heard the expression, "Get your blood moving." Well, that's exactly what you're doing here. Your energy shifts as you move your body. You'll feel refreshed and renewed.

2. Breathe Fully

Being bombarded with many demands and different emotions from others during the day influences your emotional energy and can cause it to get stuck in an undesirable emotional state. If you find that you're frustrated, overwhelmed, or angry, it's likely that the stuck energy is showing up for you as shallow breathing (from your chest only).

Changing your breathing pattern can immediately shift your energy. Sitting up straight with your feet flat on the floor, place one hand just below your chest and the other on your lower abdomen. Keep your mouth closed. Inhale slowly, expanding throughout your rib cage and stomach. Pause one to two seconds. Exhale slowly making your exhalation a bit longer than your inhalation. Pause one to two seconds. Use your hands to feel your chest and stomach move as you breathe.

Repeat this deep breathing pattern for ten or more breaths. As you do, you'll start to notice a "settling down" of energy from your head into your body (you can actually feel this happening). As a result, you'll become more relaxed, peaceful, and centered. This is why meditation, yoga, and even running are so beneficial. They all ask you to breathe more deeply, which has a calming effect on your nervous system and emotions, and helps to bring you back into a balanced state.

Moving stuck energy and shifting energy may be new concepts for you. Energy is very subtle to detect. By starting to become aware of it, you'll find it much easier to manage your mental energy (thoughts and states of mind) and emotional energy (feelings) rather than having these energies control you.

Begin to experiment with sensing energy, and practice these two powerful ways to shift your energy. Whether you move your body or breathe fully, you'll see a quick and positive change in how you feel. Try it, and be open to the new.

"Things come suitable to their time."

—ENID BAGNOLD

47

THE MAGIC OF SPONTANEOUS COMBUSTION

O NE OF MY FAVORITE EPISODES from the comedy television show *Everybody Loves Raymond* (originally broadcast by CBS) illustrates a great example of knowing when it's time to walk away from a task and do something else, in order to uncover the steps needed to finish the original task.

Raymond is a sportswriter facing a deadline, and he's having trouble finishing his article. He called his wife to say that he wasn't going to make it home for dinner. His wife wanted to help by doing something nice for him so she brought his dinner to the sports room. Much to her surprise—and to Raymond's horror—she found him playing cards with his buddies. Well, you can imagine the looks on both of their faces as Raymond says, "But I'm working!" And the truth is, he was. He was working…from the inside out. He had found the secret to achieving success through the magic of spontaneous combustion.

> *Answers magically appear through "incubating and percolating."*

I can totally relate to Raymond's story. There are times when no matter how often I go over something, I just can't seem to come up with the answer. The more I try to think creatively, the more elusive the solution becomes. When I realize that sinking my teeth deeper into the situation will only bring more frustration and wasted time, I let go of the task at hand and do something else instead. And once I walk away, I inevitably receive my answers.

Some answers come to me at the oddest times—when I'm driving, in the shower, while running, in meditation, unloading the dishwasher, dancing, or having dinner with friends. Even though it looks like I'm not working, in reality I am. It's just at a different level of consciousness. Let's go back to Raymond to show you what I mean.

Raymond was "working" while playing cards through "incubating and percolating." He was incubating by putting himself into a relaxing environment where his thinking process could go underground and work at a subconscious level. While incubating, his subconscious mind began percolating with thoughts, ideas, and solutions. Over time, they bubbled up into his conscious mind as creative inspiration. Even though it seemed as if the answers magically appeared without any conscious effort on his part, they were really the result of spontaneous combustion through incubating and percolating. In other words:

JEANNE SHARBUNO

Walking Away + Relaxing + Incubating + Percolating + Time = The Magic of Spontaneous Combustion

When you find yourself reaching an impasse with something you're working on, walk away from it. Enjoy doing something else while your subconscious mind is at work incubating and percolating. Be pleasantly surprised as your answers or solutions suddenly appear when you least expect them. Now go back to your task and finish it up with ease. You've just achieved success through the magic of spontaneous combustion. Delight in its magic as you let it work in your life.

"There are two ways of spreading light—to be the candle or the mirror that reflects it."

—EDITH WHARTON

48

WHAT YOUR MIRROR REFLECTION IS TELLING YOU

BEING IN RELATIONSHIP WITH OTHERS is an excellent way to learn how to live success…from the inside out by utilizing the tool, "what your mirror reflection is telling you." This can be very challenging as it brings your focus back to you, rather than keeping it on the people or circumstances outside of you. This isn't always easy, and you may not be up for this kind of self-reflection. That's why this is an advanced tool to use in accelerating growth and success.

The people you relate with reflect back to you the things you need to know about yourself—especially if they've triggered a strong emotional reaction in you. Often, this mirror reflection is showing you the very thing you need to change or heal in yourself, rather than blaming others and expecting them to change. It's telling you to look within, rather than without.

Here's an example from a group perspective:

A leadership team I'm working with was discussing the poor attitudes of some of their employees. The employees' behavior was of legitimate concern. Yet what really struck me was that some of the leadership team's attitudes were very similar to those of the employees they were talking about. What they haven't realized yet is that their employees are reflecting back to them their very own behavior.

The message for the leadership team is to look in the mirror at themselves and make a change within themselves first. The question is whether they're up for the challenge to do so. It's much easier to look externally and say the employees have to change, rather than taking personal responsibility to internally change as a leadership team. If they change on the inside first, the outside circumstances can't help but change.

Here's another example of "what your mirror reflection is telling you:"

A client was having great difficulty in working with one of his colleagues. One day my client said, "He always makes me so mad." Rather than continue to focus on what his colleague was doing, I asked him to look within himself to see why he kept having such a strong emotional reaction to this man. Usually when there's lots of emotional charge around an interaction, it has to do with something from the past rather than with the person in the present. His colleague was reflecting back to him something he needed to learn.

After much soul-searching, he realized that this man reminded him of his older brother and the sibling rivalry they had when they were young. This current time experience was giving him the opportunity to become aware of and heal some old emotional wounds he was still carrying around. Once my client did this internal work, his colleague no longer bothered him like he had in the past.

> *When you change on the inside, the outside circumstances can't help but change.*

"What your mirror reflection is telling you" is an invaluable tool to accelerate your growth and success. It takes courage to come back and look at yourself to see where you need to change. However, the rewards are worth it. The next time you find yourself wanting the other person to change or reacting strongly to a situation, ask yourself this, "What is my mirror reflection telling me?" and then act on it.

"The world is full of genies waiting to grant your wishes."

—PERCY ROSS

49

A SECRET TO SUCCESS AND HAPPINESS

IF YOU WANT TO HAVE A SATISFYING and fulfilling life, then you must learn how to ask for what you want. Percy Ross says, "You've got to ask! Asking is, in my opinion, the world's most powerful—and neglected—secret to success and happiness."

Asking for what you want is a skill to be mastered. You may already be very good at it, or you may need some improvement in this area, or you may need to learn how to ask. Where do you find yourself along this continuum of asking for what you want?

A client found out exactly where she was not long ago. She had just returned from a ski trip with an interesting insight. One of the men in the group was always asking for what he wanted. For instance, when he wasn't happy with the condo he'd been assigned, he went to the office, explained why it wasn't suitable, and asked for a different one. He was then given an upgrade at the same price with a magnificent view.

> *Asking for what you want is a skill to be mastered.*

My client was impressed when this man relayed his story to the group. She said, "I would've just put up with it. It wouldn't have even occurred to me to ask for something else." Over the week, she watched him continue to ask for what he wanted and found she was becoming increasingly irritated with him. When she looked closer, she realized she was irritated with herself instead. What he was doing was reflecting back to her a skill and a behavior she wanted for herself.

"Ask for what you want" became one of her new goals. She read *The Aladdin Factor* by Jack Canfield and Mark Victor Hansen, a book about how to ask for what you want, and began implementing the suggested tips. She found that she didn't always know what she wanted and took steps to gain more clarity so she could be specific in her asking. She realized that she had to look at and change her beliefs around worthiness and deservingness in order to have what she asked for. And, she found it took work to ask for what she wanted—work that resulted in sweet rewards.

There are many people waiting to give you what you want. However, you must ask for it. Remember: this is a skill. And the best way to learn it, improve it, or master it is to be aware of what you want and then ask for it. Wherever you are on this continuum, start practicing this powerful secret to success and happiness by asking for 5 to 10 things that you want this week. Set yourself up for success by asking for the small things first. Notice how you feel when you ask—and when you receive.

Percy Ross says, "The world is full of genies waiting to grant your wishes." Help them to help you, and remember to ask.

"You give birth to that on which you fix your mind."

—ANTOINE DE SAINT-EXUPERY

50

TEN EMPOWERING MESSAGES TO TELL YOURSELF DAILY

~~~~~

WHAT YOU LISTEN TO AND WHAT YOU SAY to yourself can make all the difference between having a great day and a not so great day.

If you listen to the news while getting ready for work and then again while driving into the office, you've already received many negative messages before your day has hardly begun. Not to mention what your colleagues, clients, or boss may greet you with once you arrive. These negative messages can be so insidious that you're not even aware of how they're affecting you. And then of course, there's your own self-talk, which may not be as supportive as it could be.

That's why it's so important to have in place a personal framework of empowering messages which can help counteract the negative energy you're constantly bombarded with. By reminding yourself of these messages daily, you'll put yourself into a state of being that is favorable to achieving success, joy, and fulfillment—despite outside influences. And, you'll have created for yourself a set of principles that

> *Put yourself into a state of being that is favorable to achieving success, joy, and fulfillment.*

can powerfully guide you and support you…from the inside out.

Here are ten empowering messages for you to follow. They may be just right for you, or you may want to make some changes so they are more relevant and personal.

TEN EMPOWERING MESSAGES TO TELL YOURSELF DAILY

1. Trust your instincts
2. Do your best
3. Count your blessings
4. Less is more
5. Monitor your thoughts
6. Acknowledge others often
7. Ask for help when you need it
8. Rest in solutions
9. Attitude is everything
10. Stop and smell the roses

Once you decide what your ten empowering messages are going to be, put them in a place where you can see them often (mine are framed and sitting on my desk). Keeping them visible can mean the difference between slipping into a funk because you just got off a challenging call or being energized to pick up the phone again.

Let these messages be your ten daily reminders—your snippets of profound advice—your empowering self-talk. Let them create for you a supportive and positive mental environment that will shape your attitudes and behaviors for success, and guide the actions you choose to take. Let your ten empowering messages…make your day.

"May you look back on the past with as much pleasure as you look forward to the future."

—PAUL DICKSON

51

A POWERFUL EXERCISE TO WRAP UP THE YEAR

THE END OF THE YEAR IS RAPIDLY APPROACHING, and the holiday season is now upon us. What is your normal modus operandi at this time of the year? Do you take time to reflect on the year just ending? Or do you get caught up in the hustle bustle of the holidays, forget what happened during the year, and jump right into the New Year on the run?

As the year draws to a close, one of the most valuable things you can do for yourself is to reflect on all the wonderful things that took place for you during the year, to accept and let go of all the things that didn't go as well as you would have liked, to acknowledge your growth and the changes the past year has brought you, and to appreciate who it is you've become as a person. This reflection, this going within process, is a part of living success…from the inside out.

Here is an exercise to help you reflect on your life and to wrap up the year just ending:

WRAPPING UP THE YEAR, AN EXERCISE

> *When you reflect on and complete the year just ending, you open up a space for yourself to bring wonderful things to you in the New Year.*

1. Getting Ready

Find 30 to 60 minutes just for you. Go to a comfortable place that is quiet and where you'll be undisturbed. Put on some soft music. Have your favorite comfort food and beverage nearby.

2. Acknowledge Your Accomplishments

Make a list of 10 to 20 things you've accomplished this year. They can either be big or small things like getting promoted, eliminating debt, cleaning out the garage (finally!), a new job, helping your child, learning something new, taking your dream vacation, giving up a bad habit, starting an exercise routine, etc.

These are your wins and successes for the year. If you need some help to jog your memory, browse through your calendar month by month. Relish the richness of your life as you remember the year. Pat yourself on the back for all you've done. Be proud of your accomplishments, your growth, and your changes.

3. Tie Up Loose Ends

Make a list of 10 to 20 things that you've left unfinished or that are incomplete. These might be projects, tasks, having that difficult conversation with a co-worker or family member, ending a relationship, updating your resume, hanging on to disappointments that are keeping you from moving forward, etc. Put an asterisk next to the ones you want to complete and a check mark next to those you have no desire or intention of completing.

Next, decide when you're going to complete the things you really do want to finish. Will it be before the end of the year, or will they be goals for the New Year? Whatever it is, commit fully to making this happen.

Lastly, accept the things you don't want to complete and give yourself permission to let them go once and for all. Feel the weight come off your shoulders as you accept and let go of this unfinished business. The very act of doing so is your way of completing these things. Congratulate yourself for not carrying this dead weight with you into the New Year.

4. Celebration

Here is the fun part. This is where you honor yourself by doing something special to acknowledge the end of another year in your life's journey. Go out and do something great to celebrate your successes, what you've let go of, the new people in your life, the shifts you've made, everything and anything that the year has brought for you. You can do this alone or with others. The key is to consciously choose an activity for the sole purpose of celebration. Schedule it into your calendar right away. Make your celebration fun and festive.

As you bring a close to the year, let yourself feel the joy and deep satisfaction for who it is you've become as a person. By taking the time to reflect on and complete the year just ending, you are actually creating space for yourself—emotionally, mentally, physically, and spiritually—to bring wonderful things to you in the New Year. Go ahead and treat yourself this holiday season. Give yourself the gift of "Wrapping Up the Year."

"The challenge is to be yourself in a world that is trying to make you like everyone else."

—RENEE LOCKS

52

WORDS TO INSPIRE...
A GRADUATION
MESSAGE

WHEN I RECEIVED AN INVITATION to my cousin's high school graduation, it occurred to me that graduation isn't only about graduating from school. It can also be about graduating from a certain phase in life. Or about graduating to a higher level of understanding in living life.

These graduations deserve our congratulations and acknowledgment too. All of us are graduating in some way. I'd like to share with you the graduation message I wrote to my cousin. My sharing it is also my tribute to her. Perhaps you'll find meaning in it for yourself or for someone close to you.

> *When you come from your truth and your heart's desire, you will have real happiness.*

✶ ✶ ✶ ✶ ✶ ✶

DEAR WENDY,

As you step out into the world, you may find that there will be people who want you to be just like them. Those who will want you to think, be, speak, and act as they do. That is about who they are, not about who you are. Stay true to yourself, Wendy. To what's most important to you, to what's right for you. Acting from your own integrity takes great courage. And, you will be constantly challenged. Yet by coming from your truth and your heart's desire, you will have real happiness.

I'm reminded of a quote by Renee Locks, "The challenge is to be yourself in a world that is trying to make you like everyone else." Rise to this challenge, rather than let it get you down. Always remember Wendy, that you are very unique with your own special inner brilliance. Let it shine through you day after day. It is a gift you give to yourself, your family, those close to you, and the community you'll serve.

There are many of us behind you who are loving you and supporting you as you begin this new stage in your life. Know that you are not alone. Know that you *are blessed. Know that you are good enough. Know that the world is a much better place for you being in it.*

My wish for you is that your 18th year, your graduation, your college years, and the years beyond will bring you a wondrous song in your heart and a lively dance in your step. You are a very special young woman, Wendy. May all your dreams and more come true.

LOVE, JEANNE

✶ ✶ ✶ ✶ ✶ ✶

My wish for you is the same. You are to be acknowledged and congratulated for your graduation. As you move on to the next level in the school of life, let these words linger in your heart and help you to live success…from the inside out. Words to inspire…a graduation message.

ADDITIONAL READING

Cameron, Julia. *The Artist's Way: A Spiritual Path to Higher Creativity.* New York: Jeremy P. Tarcher/Perigee Books, 1992.

Canfield, Jack and Hansen, Mark Victor. *The Aladdin Factor.* New York: Berkley Publishing Group, 1995.

Chu, Chin-Ning. *Do Less, Achieve More: Discover the Hidden Power of Giving In.* New York: HarperCollins Publishers, 2000.

Ditzler, Jinny S. *Your Best Year Yet: Ten Questions for Making the Next Twelve Months Your Most Successful Ever.* New York: Warner Books, 2000.

Hill, Napoleon. *Think and Grow Rich.* North Hollywood, CA: Wilshire Book Co., Revised Edition, 1999.

Johnson, Spencer. *Who Moved My Cheese? An Amazing Way to Deal With Change in Your Work and in Your Life.* New York: Putnam Publishing Group, 1998.

Kabat-Zinn, Jon. *Wherever You Go, There You Are: Mindfulness Meditation in Everyday Life.* New York: Hyperion, 1995.

Ponder, Catherine. *The Dynamic Laws of Prosperity.* Marina del Ray, CA: Devorss & Co., Revised 1998.

Robbins, Anthony. *Awaken the Giant Within: How to Take Immediate Control of Your Mental, Emotional, Physical, and Financial Destiny.* New York: Fireside, 1992.

Roman, Sanaya. *Living With Joy: Keys to Personal Power and Spiritual Transformation.* Tiburon, CA: H J Kramer, 1986.

Sheerer, Robin A. *No More Blue Modays: Four Keys to Finding Fulfillment at Work.* Palo Alto, CA: Davies-Black, 1999.

Tieger, Paul D. and Barron-Tieger, Barbara. *Do What You Are: Discover the Perfect Career for You Through the Secrets of Personality Type.* Boston, New York, Toronto, London: Little, Brown and Co., revised 2001.

Winter, Barbara J. *Making a Living Without A Job: Winning Ways for Creating Work That You Love.* New York: Bantam Books, 1993.

ABOUT THE AUTHOR

JEANNE SHARBUNO is a career facilitator, workshop leader, and corporate consultant with a 20-year background in sales, marketing, and management.

Since founding **Step Up! Success** in 1997, Jeanne has developed and led workshops on career issues, personal effectiveness, goal setting, strategic planning, and train-the-coach programs. She has facilitated support groups for people in career transition, entrepreneurs, and small business leadership teams. She has also provided outplacement consulting for downsized employees and coached hundreds of people in career-life planning. A partial list of her clients include AT&T, Brinks, Xerox, Unity Church, and numerous smaller businesses and professional associations.

As author of **Success...From the Inside Out!** a monthly e-mail newsletter, Jeanne has gained an international following and many diverse clients seeking career and professional development coaching. A dynamic speaker, she is frequently sought after as a presenter and workshop leader.

Jeanne has been awarded the distinguished Professional Certified Coach (PCC) designation from the International Coach Federation.

She has studied for over eight years with a meditation teacher from Malaysia and is strongly committed to a daily meditation practice. An avid and award-winning ballroom dancer, Jeanne lives in Atlanta, Georgia.

AN INVITATION

TO LEARN MORE ABOUT the various resources Jeanne provides, call (770) 315-4574 or send an e-mail to insideout@jeannesharbuno.com.

Resources include:
- Presentations, seminars, and workshops
- Career and professional development coaching; in-person or telephone
- Best Year Yet goal-setting and strategic planning workshops with follow-up implementation support for teams and individuals
- *Success…From the Inside Out!* a free monthly e-mail newsletter. To subscribe, send a blank e-mail to: success_insideout-subscribe@topica.email-publisher.com

"Empowering people to live success…from the inside out"

Jeanne Sharbuno
(770) 315-4574
insideout@jeannesharbuno.com

INDEX

"have to" 147, 148
"should" 123, 147, 148

A

abundance 76, 114, 115, 117, 118, 119
accelerate xxi, 235
accelerating growth 233
accept xx, 36, 247, 249
accessible 85
accomplishment 48, 155, 156, 157, 215, 248
accountability 182
achieve xx, xxii, 8, 57, 70, 156, 187, 193, 199, 200, 215, 229, 257
    achievement 156, 193
acknowledge xiii, 18, 108, 109, 127, 128, 155, 156, 170, 171, 195, 244, 247, 248, 249, 255
    acknowledge others often 127, 244
    acknowledgements 127
action xxi, xxii, 14, 22, 61, 62, 70, 140, 181, 183, 195, 199, 200, 212, 216, 244
action steps xxi, 62, 183
addicted 41

adrenaline
    adrenaline junkie 41, 44
    adrenaline quiz 41, 42
    adrenaline, running on 41, 43
advanced style of relating 128
advanced tool 233
affirmations 118
afraid xvii, 22, 66, 175, 211, 212
agenda 203
Aladdin Factor, The (Canfield and Hansen) 240
aligned 131, 132
alignment 131, 132
angels next door 188, 189
anger 36, 131, 170
answers 17, 18, 25, 44, 85, 86, 104, 108, 188, 212, 228, 229
appreciation xiii, 114, 118, 155, 156
approach, creative 139
Artist's Way, The (Cameron) 52, 97, 152
as it is within, so it is without xx, 135, 136
ask for help when you need it 44, 69, 70, 244
ask for what you want 199, 239, 240
assistance 176, 177, 189
attention 18, 19, 22, 61, 62, 85, 98, 113, 119, 124, 135, 139, 140, 203, 204
attitude is everything 244
attitudes 14, 234, 244

B
baby steps 48, 98, 99
backpack of your life 8
balance 156, 221, 222, 223

balanced state 222, 223
barometer 86
behaviors 244
being
    being, state of 243, 244
    Being + Doing + Having 1
    beings, creative 51
belief system xx, 56
beliefs 117, 118, 240
bigger game, playing a 81
blaming 233
blessings 113, 114, 244
bliss 25, 26
block 194, 212
blocks 212
body 21, 22, 44, 52, 86, 152, 221, 222, 223
    body emotions 42, 86
    body sensation 86
    body wisdom 21, 22
boredom 132
brainstorm 140, 171
breath 18, 22, 221, 222, 223
breathe 222, 223
    breathing 18, 21, 22, 222
    breathing pattern 222
bridges, building 147, 148
burn-out 41
burned-out 151
business xv, 99, 119, 127, 151, 155, 171, 204, 215, 216, 249, 259
    business, home-based 171
busyness 17, 108

C

call to action 199, 200
calming effect 222, 223
Cameron, Julie 49, 52, 97, 152, 257
Canfield, Jack 240, 257
career 22, 104, 123, 129, 169, 170, 171, 175, 176, 177, 203, 204, 258, 259, 261
    career change 169, 170, 171, 175, 177
    career planning 176
    career services 177
    career transition 104, 176, 259
caretaking role 165
caring 208
catalyst 140, 177
centered 18, 118, 222
challenge xix, xx, 56, 80, 140, 234, 251, 254
    challenged 254
change xv, xx, xxii, 21, 62, 91, 92, 101, 118, 119, 131, 136, 156, 167, 169, 170, 176, 177, 183, 188, 221, 223, 233, 234, 235, 240, 244, 247, 248, 257
circumstances xx, 208, 233, 234, 235
clarity 2, 240
clues 21, 22, 131
clutter 7, 8, 9
coach xiii, xv, xvii, xix, xx, xxi, xxii, 8, 51, 109, 117, 118, 165, 177, 182, 188, 194, 195, 200, 259, 261
    Coach U 43
    coaching iii, v, xix, xxi, xxii, 8, 51, 117, 118, 165, 200, 259, 261
comfort 75, 93, 99, 199, 248
    comfort zone 199
commit xv, xx, 3, 127, 144, 152, 183, 249, 260

commitment xiii, 44, 79, 171, 182
communicate 35, 36, 37, 147
    communicating 147
    communication 35, 124, 147, 148
    communication, art of 35
company-initiated restructuring 169
comparing 194, 195
    comparison blues xviii, 193. 194, 195
    comparison blues antidote 195
completion, create
compliment 127
concept 93, 139
    concepts xxi, xxii, 223
confidence 132, 156, 212
conflict 22, 35
    conflict, resolution 22, 35
connecting 208
connection 51, 109, 151, 182
    connection, spiritual 109
conscious
    conscious effort 118, 228
    conscious mind 228
    consciousness 25, 118, 119, 171, 228
    consciousness, level of 228
consultants 71
contemplate 17
    contemplation 108
continuum 239, 240
conventional wisdom 86
count your blessings 114, 244
courage 93, 109, 127, 144, 199, 200, 235, 254

create space 8
created the space 30
creating space 249
creative
    creative approach 139
    creative beings 51
    creative inspiration 228
    creative process 52
    creative thinking 139
creativity xiii, 23, 25, 49, 51, 52, 140
criticism 156
criticized 211
cultivating 155, 157

D

daily reminders 244
daily three, the 55, 56, 57
day-to-day xx, 108
day-to-day life 17, 76
de-motivated 215
deadline 42, 47, 211, 215, 227
deepest desires 109
delegate 30
deserve 43, 132, 166, 170, 253
deservingness 240
desire 56, 80, 109, 124, 173, 182, 204, 211, 249, 254
directions 52, 87
discipline 199, 200
discouraged 215
disharmony 147
do your best 162, 244

do-ability 99
drain 7, 8, 139
dream xiii, 22, 75, 92, 97, 98, 99, 103, 104, 105, 107, 108, 109, 127, 248, 255
    dream list 108
    dreams 92, 104, 107, 108, 109, 255
dwelling 139, 140, 170
Dynamic Laws of Prosperity, The 118, 258

E

ease 30, 124, 167, 169, 171, 175, 177, 181, 212, 229
effectiveness xxii, 124, 144, 259
eliminate 7, 8, 9, 44, 148, 166, 175
    eliminate, what drains you 7, 8
emotion
    emotional charge 234
    emotional energy 221, 222, 223
    emotional reaction 233, 234
    emotional state 222
    emotional survival kit 169, 171, 175, 177
    emotional wounds 235
    emotionally 36, 41, 43, 166, 249
    emotionally charged 36
employee assistance programs 176
empowering messages 136, 243, 244
energy 7, 8, 13, 14, 41, 80, 113, 123, 139, 148, 166, 219, 221, 222, 223, 243
    energy drainer 139
    energy fields 13
    energy level 7, 113
    energy, sense your 223

energy, sensing your 223
energy, shifting 223
enjoyment 75
enthusiasm 156
environment 8, 29, 127, 131, 170, 183, 228, 244
essence 104, 108, 182
excellence 162, 209, 211, 212
exercises
    Exercise: How to Recognize Success in "Failure" 216, 217
    Exercise: Trust Yourself 86, 87
    Exercise: Wrapping Up the Year 246, 247
expand 114, 222
expansive 124
experience xiii, xix, 26, 56, 61, 65, 75, 87, 113, 170, 176, 207, 235
experts 70, 71
external world 119
externally 234

F

failure xviii, 56, 66, 92, 199, 211, 215, 216, 217
fatigue 21, 131, 165, 221
fear 65, 66, 69, 91, 170, 175, 199, 211, 212
    fear of failure 66
    fear of looking stupid 66
    fear of not being good enough 66
    fear of not being perfect 66
    fear of success 66
    fear of taking a risk 66
    fear trap 175
filling the form (tool) 97, 98, 99
finances 175, 177

financial planner 177
fine-tune 183
fine-tuning 124
flourish 128, 194
flow 23, 25, 26, 86, 87, 140, 147, 183, 204
    flow activities 25, 26
focus xxi, 29, 31, 43, 113, 114, 117, 118, 119, 127, 135, 136, 140, 155, 156, 165, 166, 170, 203, 215, 216, 233, 234
forbidden joy 75
freedom 92, 167, 197, 212
from the inside out xiii, xv, xvii, xviii, xix, xx, xxi, xxii, 1, 2, 3, 13, 17, 22, 25, 29, 31, 37, 41, 47, 52, 56, 62, 66, 69, 76, 85, 87, 98, 104, 109, 114, 119, 123, 124, 128, 132, 136, 139, 147, 152, 156, 162, 166, 169, 183, 189, 194, 199, 204, 207, 208, 211, 216, 221, 227, 233, 244, 247, 255, 259, 261
fruits of your thoughts 119
frustrated xix, 56, 62, 151, 165, 222
frustration 131, 139, 228
fulfilled 55, 56, 108, 109, 124
fulfillment 87, 109, 124, 132, 182, 243, 244
fun xviii, xx, xxii, 25, 26, 51, 52, 103, 119, 123, 132, 151, 152, 166, 182, 199, 204, 249

G

gifts 2, 51, 108, 194, 195
giving thanks 114
goal
    goal, "Heart" 124
    goal, "Should" 123
    goal-setting xviii, 123, 124, 261
Goal Filter, The xviii, 123, 124

graduation xviii, 253, 255
gratitude 113, 114
guidance 85, 87, 189
guide xv, xvii, 104, 204, 244
guiding 86, 188, 204
gut feelings 85, 86
gut instincts 131

H

habit 7, 43, 44, 128, 139, 152, 199, 200, 248
Hansen, Mark Victor 240, 257
happiness 30, 114, 167, 239, 240, 254
harmoniously 147
health 26, 114
heart xiii, xviii, 17, 26, 36, 37, 56, 57, 59, 76, 108, 114, 123, 124, 173, 182, 205, 208, 212, 254, 255
heart's desire 124, 182, 254
Higher Power 109, 182, 188, 189
home-based business 171
human spirit 207

I

improvement 212, 239
incubating 228, 229
individual effort 187
inner
    inner compass 85, 86, 87, 188
    inner knowing 86
    inner resolve 80
    inner self 188
    inner strength 109, 207

inner voice 17
innovative xxi, 29, 55, 57
inside out xiii, xviii, xix, xx, xxi, xxii, 1, 3, 13, 17, 22, 25, 29, 31, 37, 41, 47, 52, 56, 62, 69, 76, 85, 87, 98, 104, 109, 114, 119, 128, 132, 136, 139, 147, 152, 156, 162, 166, 169, 183, 189, 194, 199, 204, 207, 208, 211, 216, 233, 247, 255, 259, 261
    inside-out approach 37, 38
insight xx, 136, 239
inspiration xix, 135
    inspiration, creative 228
    inspired xiii, xix, 124
    inspires 128
    inspiring 91, 127, 212
    inspiring words 91
instinctively 47, 85
instincts 85, 86, 244
    instincts, trusting your 86, 244
integrity 254
intention xvi, 79, 182, 249
interaction 208, 234
interactions 208
internal
    internal guidance system 85, 87
    internal strength 182
    internal work 235
    internal world 119
    internally 234
interviewing techniques 176
intuition 69, 85, 86, 124, 131, 188
    intuitive goal-setting 124
irresistibly attractive xvii, 13, 14

irritated 30, 42, 240

J

joy xviii, 22, 23, 25, 26, 30, 51, 52, 56, 75, 87, 109, 113, 114, 124, 132, 143, 144, 203, 208, 243, 244, 249, 258
Joy of Moseying xviii, 143, 144
judgment 148

K

key xviii, xx, 56, 69, 70, 71, 86, 124, 183, 216, 249, 258
knowledge 70, 176

L

lack 42, 117, 118, 119
    lacking 61, 65, 143
language 148
leadership 151, 234
    leadership team 234, 259
learn xviii, xxi, 19, 47, 56, 65, 85, 86, 92, 107, 135, 136, 175, 216, 217, 233, 234, 239, 240, 248, 261
leisure 52, 143
less is more 55, 56, 244
let go 75, 76, 166, 212, 217, 228, 247, 249
level of consciousness 228
life purpose
like attracts like 13, 14, 117
listen to the messages 204
listening 17, 18, 21, 22, 43, 52, 62, 109, 203
livelihood 207
Living with Joy (Roman, Sanaya) 114, 258
living your dreams 109

Locks, Renee 251, 254
loss 132, 167, 208
love xviii, 2, 75, 91, 92, 114, 128, 182
luxury 75, 76, 108
    luxury, simple xvii, xviii, 75, 76

M
mantra 140, 162
master 240
mastered 239, 240
mastering 35, 143
Mayberry Mosey 144
meaningful 2, 131, 132, 183
meditate 17, 182
meditation xix, 108, 189, 222, 228, 257, 260
mental
    mental energy 221, 223
    mental fatigue 221
    mentally 41, 43, 114, 166, 249
mentor 131, 188, 195
messages 21, 22, 108, 136, 203, 204, 243, 244
mind 25, 36, 123, 133, 152, 176, 182, 194, 211, 215, 221, 223, 229, 241
    mind's eye 80
    mindset 56, 79, 80, 81
mini-spring breaks 151, 152
mirror 14, 162, 231, 233, 234, 235
    mirror reflection 233, 234, 235
mission 47, 48, 107
modus operandi 247
momentum 80, 140
money 1, 2, 43, 103, 117, 118, 119, 175, 182

money, beliefs 117, 118
money, relationship with 117, 118, 119
monitor your thoughts 170, 171, 244
moseying xviii, 143, 144
motivated 181
motivation 156, 182
movement 221

N
natural gifts, talents 51
natural law 117, 118
needs xvii, 91, 165
negative 14, 61, 113, 136, 148, 156, 166, 170, 243
    negative energy 14, 243
    negative expectancy 79, 81
    negative thoughts 170, 171
    negativity 113
nervous system 169, 221, 223
neutral frame of mind 36
neutral place 36
nurturing 76

O
on-line career programs 176
open heart 36
opportunity 235
order xxi, 55, 91, 99, 119, 216, 227, 240
organize 55, 57
outcome 79, 80
outer self 188
outside in 1, 3

overwhelming 9, 48, 70, 97
ownership 36

P

panic zone 199
passionate 51, 131, 132
past 2, 36, 143, 207, 234, 235, 245, 247
patience xiii, 44
peace 42, 107, 109, 114
peace of mind 176, 182
peaceful 222
perceived 216
percolating 228, 229
perfect 13, 37, 91, 161, 162, 211, 212
    perfection 162, 209, 211, 212
    perfectionism 161, 162, 211, 212
    perfectionist 161
permission xx, 43, 56, 166, 249
personal framework 243
personal responsibility 234
personality 22, 258
perspective xx, xxi, 136, 234
perspectives 37
physically 43, 166, 249
physically, mentally, and emotionally 41, 43, 166
play 13, 26, 80, 81, 107, 140, 152, 203
    playful 76, 152
    playing 52, 152, 227, 228
    playing a bigger game 80
pleasure 75, 76, 245
    pleasure, simple 76

point of reference 86
Ponder, Catherine 118, 258
positive xv, 14, 79, 80, 81, 113, 114, 136, 140, 148, 170, 221, 223
    positive attitude 170
    postive energy
    positive expectancy 79, 80, 81
    positive mental environment 170, 244
    positive thoughts 136, 170
possibilities 140, 170, 171
power 105, 203, 204, 219, 257, 258
practice 17, 35, 36, 55, 97, 114, 118, 128, 156, 162, 199, 200, 208, 223, 260
praise 155, 156
pray 182
prayer 189
present 37, 234
presents 30
principle of responsibility 36
principles, set of 243
priorities 2, 55, 56, 216, 217
problem xix, xx, 17, 25, 52, 62, 117, 139, 140, 194
    problem-solving, creative approach 139, 140
    problems xix, 14, 43, 137, 139
process 2, 3, 23, 35, 69, 98, 104, 123, 152, 171, 182, 183, 204, 216, 228, 247
    process, creative 52
procrastinating 47, 62, 65, 66, 211, 212
    procrastination xxii, 61, 62, 65, 66, 69, 70, 71, 211, 212
    procrastination, as foe 61, 62, 65, 66, 69, 70
    procrastination, as friend 61, 62, 65, 66, 69, 70
    procrastination, blast through 66, 69, 71

    procrastination, blasting tips 70, 71
    procrastination, underlying source 65, 66, 69
productive 55, 139, 152
productivity 144
prosperity 118, 119
prosperity consciousness 118, 119
purpose 249
purpose in life xx
putting yourself first 165, 166

R

racking my brain for ideas 98
re-connect 51, 52
re-entry 181, 182, 183
re-evaluate 216, 217
re-focus 18
re-group 216, 217
reality 79, 98, 99, 175, 183, 195, 228
refine 182
reflect 14, 17, 62, 132, 216, 231, 233, 247, 248, 249
reflection xxii, 62, 108, 183, 233, 235, 247
reframe 170
refreshed 25, 222
rejuvenates 76
relationship 7, 99, 117, 118, 119, 233, 248
    relationship with money 117, 118, 119
    relationships xv, 8, 52, 123
relax 29, 152
    relaxation 151
    relaxed 18, 222
    relaxing 25, 26, 228, 229

renewed 222
resistance 211, 212
resources 169, 176, 261
responsibilities 17, 76
rest in solutions 139, 140, 244
result 47, 66, 80, 91, 132, 212, 222, 228
    results xxii, 31, 47, 48, 56, 86, 140, 162, 170, 182, 183, 199, 200
resume writing 176
revise 216, 217
rewards xv, 2, 9, 235, 240
risk 37, 91, 92, 93, 97, 98, 99, 132, 155
    risk-taking 93, 97, 98
    risks 92, 93
Rogers, Will 89, 93
Roman, Sanaya 11, 111, 114, 258
Ross, Percy 237, 239, 240

S

salary 176
    salary negotiation 176
say no 30, 44, 166
say yes 3, 30
scarcity 113, 118
self 21, 51, 52, 92, 188, 189
    self-care xxii, 166
    self-confidence 132, 156
    self-expression 52
    self-fulfilling prophecy 135, 170
    self-talk 170, 243, 244
sensing energy 223

set of principles 243
shallow breathing 21, 222
shifting energy 223
sibling rivalry 235
simple luxuries xvii, xviii, 75, 76
simple pleasure 76
simplicity xv, 55
skill
    skill, asking for what you want 239
    skill, trusting yourself 85, 86
    skills training, interviewing techniques 176
    skills training, resume writing 176
    skills training, salary negotiation 176
    skills, transferable 176
small steps 47, 48, 69, 70, 71
smile 114, 157, 205, 207, 208
smooth re-entry 182, 183
solution 25, 140, 228
    solutions xix, 139, 140, 228, 229
    solutions, creative 140
    solutions, external 228, 229
    solutions, rest in 139, 140, 244
soul 49, 52, 76, 125, 152, 153, 235
    soul messages 108
    soul-searching 235
space
    space, create 8
    space, created the 30
    space, creating 249
spring breaks 151, 152
spiritual connection 109

spiritually 249
spontaneous combustion 227, 228, 229
standards 161
state of being 243, 244
states of mind 221, 223
static 17
still small voice 17, 18, 26, 61, 62, 76, 188
stop and smell the roses 144, 244
strategy 165, 216
strengths 132
stress 30, 31, 76, 132, 161, 162, 176, 177
    stressed 25, 30, 165
    stressing 22
stretch 99, 183, 188, 221
    stretch zone 199, 200
struggle 124, 136
stuck 70, 91, 170, 212, 221, 222
    stuck energy 222, 223
subconscious 25, 228
    subconscious mind 228, 229
success xv, xvii, xviii, xx, xxi, xxii, 1, 2, 8, 17, 18, 26, 42, 47, 48, 56, 57, 62, 66, 79, 80, 81, 93, 97, 103, 104, 152, 155, 156, 182, 183, 187, 188, 189, 194, 199, 200, 215, 216, 217, 227, 235, 239, 240, 243, 244, 261
    success, art of appreciating 155, 156, 157
    success, fear of 66
    success ladder 103
    success, toddler method of 48
    success-minded people 187
    success...from the inside out xiii, xviii, xix, xx, xxi, xxii, 1, 3, 13, 17, 22, 25, 29, 31, 37, 41, 47, 52, 56, 62, 69, 76, 85, 87, 98, 104, 109,

114, 119, 128, 132, 136, 139, 147, 152, 156, 162, 166, 169, 183, 189, 194, 199, 204, 207, 208, 211, 216, 233, 247, 255, 259, 261
summer break 181
sumptuous living 75, 76
support xiii, 31, 109, 182, 187, 188, 244, 259, 261
    support team 189
synergy 187, 188, 189

T

take action 181
take stock 175
take the risk 37, 132
talent 125
    talents 2, 22, 51, 108, 131, 132, 194, 195
team effort 187, 189
ten seconds of boldness 199, 200
Thanksgiving 114
thinking, creative 139
thoughts
    thoughts, fruits of your 119
    thoughts, nagging 86
    thoughts, positive 136, 170
    thoughts, negative 170, 171
time 1, 2, 3, 7, 14, 17, 18, 21, 22, 25, 26, 29, 30, 35, 37, 41, 42, 43, 44, 47, 48, 52, 55, 57, 61, 62, 65, 66, 69, 70, 71, 85, 86, 93, 97, 98, 99, 104, 108, 114, 123, 131, 132, 144, 151, 152, 155, 156, 162, 163, 165, 166, 171, 175, 181, 182, 183, 200, 203, 207, 216, 225, 227, 228, 229, 235, 247, 249
    time, creating 29, 30
    time, managing 29, 30
    time, wasted 228

time waster 139
timeless 25, 26, 128
timer 26, 71
toddler method of success 48
tool kit 99
tools 169, 175, 177
    tools, career, acknowledge your emotions 170
    tools, career, consider the possibilities 170, 171
    tools, career, get expert help 177
    tools, career, monitor your thoughts 170, 171, 244
    tools, career, take stock of your finances 175
    tools, career, use available resources 176
    tools, emotional survival kit 169, 171, 175, 177
    tools, filling the form 97, 98, 99
    tools, inner compass 85, 86, 87, 188
    tools, the goal filter 123, 124
    tools, what your mirror reflection is telling you 233, 234, 235
touchstone 182
transferable skills 176
true success 103, 104
trust
    trust your instincts 86, 244
    trust yourself 83, 85, 86, 87
    trusting 85, 86, 124
    trusting yourself 85, 86
truth 66, 119, 212, 227, 254

U

unfinished business 249
unique 2, 51, 52, 194, 195, 204, 254
universe 114, 182, 203, 204

V

values 124, 131, 132
visualization 79

W

walls, building 147, 148
wasted time 228
well-being 26, 76, 152, 182
what your mirror reflection is telling you 233, 234, 235
win-win 166
wisdom xv, 21, 135, 170, 188
work 1, 8, 21, 22, 37, 42, 48, 52, 56, 62, 91, 114, 117, 119, 127, 128, 131, 132, 136, 139, 140, 144, 151, 152, 156, 161, 166, 171, 173, 176, 187, 203, 204, 207, 208, 216, 243, 258
worthiness 240

Y

yoga 222

Z

zone 26, 199
    zone, stretch 199, 200

About the Diogenes Consortium

**If you found this book thought provoking...
If you are interested in having this author...
or other of our consulting authors
design a workshop or seminar for your
company, organization, school, or team...**

Let the experienced and knowledgeable group of experts at ***The Diogenes Consortium*** go to work for you. With literally hundreds of years of combined experience in:

*Human Resources • Employee Retention
Management • Pro-Active Leadership • Teams
Encouragement • Empowerment • Motivation
Energizing • Delegating Responsibility
Spirituality in the Workplace
Presentations to start-ups and Fortune 100 companies,
tax-exempt organizations and schools
(public & private, elementary through university)
religious groups and organizations*

**Call today for a list of our
authors/speakers/presenters/consultants**

Call toll free at:
866-602-1476

Or write to us at:
2445 River Tree Circle
Sanford, FL 32771